GURU NANAK

2 INDIC VALUES SERIES

ELEANOR
NESBITT
GOPINDER
KAUR

RELIGIOUS AND MORAL EDUCATION PRESS

SERIES EDITOR:
JULIUS LIPNER

Religious and Moral Education Press
A division of SCM-Canterbury Press Ltd
a wholly owned subsidiary of Hymns Ancient & Modern Ltd
St Mary's Works, St Mary's Plain
Norwich, Norfolk NR3 3BH

© Copyright 1999, Bayeux Arts, Incorporated

Eleanor Nesbitt and Gopinder Kaur have asserted
their right under the Copyright, Designs and Patents Act, 1988
to be identified as authors of this work.

All rights reserved. No part of this publication may be
reproduced, stored in a retrieval system, or transmitted, in any
form or by any means, electronic, electrostatic, magnetic tape,
mechanical, photocopying, recording or otherwise, without
permission in writing from the publishers.

First published by Bayeux Arts Incorporated,
119 Stratton Crescent S.W., Calgary, Alberta, Canada 1999

First published in Great Britain by RMEP 1999

ISBN 1 85175 192 0

This edition is not available for sale in Canada and the U.S.A.

The publisher gratefully acknowledges the generous support of
The Alberta Foundation for the Arts and The Canada Council for the Arts

Design: Brian Dyson, Syntax Media Services

Printed in Hong Kong by King's Times Printing
for SCM-Canterbury Press Ltd, Norwich

For Rasna and Kirat with love - G
For Rachna and Manisha with love - E

Contents

Editor's preface 6
Authors' foreword 7

Chapter 1.   Who was Guru Nanak? 9
Chapter 2.   Can we really know what famous people were like? 18
Chapter 3.   Does life have a meaning? 26
Chapter 4.   Can our specific experiences teach us universal truths? 33
Chapter 5.   How do we communicate most effectively what matters most? ... 37
Chapter 6.   Are labels and uniforms necessary? 46
Chapter 7.   Are we all equal? 52
Chapter 8.   Does integrity matter? 56
Chapter 9.   Do we need a sense of direction? 62
Chapter 10. How important is wealth? 67
Chapter 11. Rituals and institutions: are they a help or a hindrance? 71
Chapter 12. How can we sum up Guru Nanak's message? 77
Chapter 13. Why end with thirteen? 81

Glossary 82
List of names and pronunciation guide 85
Acknowledgements 90
Books quoted or referred to 90
A Note for Teachers 93

Editor's Preface

The first volume of this *Series* (now renamed the *Indic Values Series*) appeared in July 1997. It is called *Sita's Story* and was published to wide acclaim. This is the second book in the *Series* and it maintains the high standards of its predecessor.

The Dharam Hinduja Institute of Indic Research (DHIIR) at Cambridge exists to undertake research into the Indic traditions according to the highest standards of scholarship and to spread the fruits of such study in a way that is relevant and useful. One of the focuses of the Institute is multicultural understanding. Both the general and particular aims of DHIIR converge marvellously in the publication of this book.

Guru Nanak was the founder of the Sikh faith; he was a man of extraordinary depth and insight. And the Sikh faith has now become a world religion both numerically and in the global distribution of its adherents. As this book will show, Guru Nanak's legacy provides much food for thought and is of universal spiritual and practical significance. The more we can appreciate and understand this legacy, the more we will be able to reap the rich rewards of intercultural understanding and mutual tolerance. That is why I hope that this book will have as wide a readership as possible—among schoolchildren, teachers, adults in different walks of life, and indeed among Sikhs who desire to gain anew from the rich resources of their faith.

The authors of this book are well-equipped to write it. Dr Eleanor Nesbitt teaches and does research in the Religions and Education Research Unit at the University of Warwick. She has a wide personal experience of South Asian faiths and communities, and has published widely on the Sikh tradition. She is a founder-member of the Punjab Research Group and an Editor of the *International Journal of Punjab Studies*. The co-author, Gopinder Kaur, herself a Sikh, graduated with a degree in French and Russian at the University of Cambridge in 1994. Since then she has worked for the crosscultural children's publisher, *Barefoot Books*. Her interest in languages and cultures has led to a keenness to explore and share her own Sikh heritage. She has undertaken postgraduate studies in Sikh scriptures at the University of London, and is co-editor of the *Sikh Bulletin*.

This year celebrates the tercentenary of the establishing of the Khalsa, or community of initiated Sikhs, and is a fitting occasion to be publishing this book.

Dr Julius Lipner,
Director, DHIIR,
University of Cambridge

Foreword

Guru Nanak's significance as an inspirational guide to life's meaning extends beyond his time (five hundred years ago) and his geographical setting (South Asia). His teachings are the basis of a world religion, Sikhism—a world religion both in the sense that Sikhs now live in substantial numbers in all the inhabited continents and in the sense that what he had to say is challenging and reassuring for people of every cultural background. It is for this reason that we decided to produce a book which would bring Guru Nanak to a new generation of readers. We decided to do this despite Guru Nanak's observation, at a time when the present-day proliferation of publications was unimaginable, that 'One may read cartloads of books...but only true understanding of the One ultimately counts; all else is the babble of the ego.'

This book aims to present Guru Nanak (often referred to respectfully as Guru Nanak Dev Ji) afresh in such a way that readers can understand his importance both sympathetically and objectively. The visual material is not incidental or decorative, but provides images that are a vital part of realising how a community, the Sikh community, has responded to Guru Nanak. The text relates his specific insights and experiences to our own contemporary concerns. So our intention is twofold—to open up people's perceptions of the Guru for discussion and reflection and to highlight the relevance of his words for today.

A well-known story relates how when Guru Nanak arrived in Multan (part of Punjab now in Pakistan) the saints and sufis there presented him with a bowl of milk, full to the brim. This he understood, in the way that it was intended, as a symbolic message to the effect that 'This place is already full to overflowing with religious teachers—we do not need any more'. Guru Nanak's immediate response was to add a white jasmine flower to the milk and hand it back. Even a country full to the brim with religious teachers could, he was indicating, be pleasantly fragranced by the Guru's word and presence.

To a world already over-filled with books, **Guru Nanak** is offered in the same spirit as that jasmine flower.

We are happy that this publication coincides with Sikhs' celebration of the tercentenary of a significant date in their history, the founding of the Khalsa. This was the formalising of the Sikh community by Guru Gobind Singh, the last of the Sikhs' human Gurus.

Eleanor Nesbitt and Gopinder Kaur,
January 1999

Painting of Guru Nanak by the Sikh artist Sobha Singh whose imaginary portraits of Guru Nanak became the best-known images of him during the 20th century.

Chapter 1: Who was Guru Nanak?

In England someone was trying to find out how young children pictured God. When he looked at their drawings he found that, although Sikhs believe that there is no image that can represent God, almost all the Sikh children in the group had drawn a man with a turban and a long white beard - just like the pictures of *Guru* Nanak which you can see in Sikhs' homes and places of worship. (Note that words which appear for the first time in **bold** type are explained in the Glossary or List of Names at the back of the book).

Here is part of a poem about Guru Nanak:

> He revealed that there is one supreme God.
> He regarded king and beggar as equal.
> He came to transform the people of the world.

If you had not seen the title of this book and this chapter, who would you think that these lines were describing? Jesus? the Prophet Mohammad? Mahatma Gandhi? In fact they were composed (in Punjabi, not English) by Bhai Gurdas. (***Bhai,*** which also means 'brother', is a title which Sikhs give to men whom they particularly respect.) Bhai Gurdas lived in the Punjab area of India in the sixteenth century, at the same time that William Shakespeare was writing plays in England, and these lines are part of a long poem which Bhai Gurdas composed in honour of Guru Nanak.

On page 13 there is a map of Punjab showing places associated with Guru Nanak's life. Notice that, although Punjab was not divided at that time, it has been since 1947, the year in which the British left India and the subcontinent was divided mainly into two independent states - India and Pakistan.

It's quite usual to come across expressions like 'fashion guru' or even 'IT guru'. Generally the word guru is written with a small 'g' and in many cases it just means a teacher or expert. In Indian languages there are no capital letters, but in English we emphasise the importance of something by using an initial capital letter.

For followers of Guru Nanak 'Guru' (with a capital 'G' in English) means a spiritual master, someone capable of driving away the darkness that so often seems to surround us. Of course the 'light' that the Guru brings is not physical, as it is when someone switches on the light in a

This postcard shows Guru Nanak surrounded by (top left to bottom left) Guru Angad, Guru Amar Das, Guru Ram Das, Guru Arjan, (top right to bottom right) Guru Hargobind, Guru Har Rai, Guru Har Krishan (the child Guru), Guru Teg Bahadar and (centre bottom) Guru Gobind Singh above the *Guru Granth Sahib* (the Guru as embodied in the scriptures).

dark room, but words like 'enlightenment' and phrases like 'seeing the light' show how readily we understand 'light' as meaning truth. As the postcard opposite illustrates, for Sikhs the title 'Guru' is reserved for Guru Nanak (1469-1539) and his ten successors plus the volume of scripture (**Guru Granth Sahib**) which has carried on guiding them since the beginning of the eighteenth century. It is also a title for God, the True Guru (**Satguru** in Punjabi).

Thus Guru Nanak was the first of the ten human Gurus whose teaching is the basis of the **Sikh** religion, although his influence has also been much wider than that. You will usually hear Sikhs refer to him as 'Guru Nanak Dev Ji', 'Dev' signifying Godliness and 'Ji' respect.

As Guru means teacher it is not surprising that the word Sikh means a learner and the Sikhs are people who follow Guru Nanak and his successors as Guru and regard as their Guru today the volume of scriptures (*Guru Granth Sahib*) which contain their message. Although speakers of English often pronounce Sikh as if it were 'seek', the Punjabi word has a short vowel (like 'pick') and ends with the sound which comes at the end of the Scottish word '*loch*'.

It is quite natural for poets and thinkers who belong to a particular faith to write enthusiastically about the great individuals who 'founded' it. Even if we aren't members of the same community we can recognise that some people have special gifts. In the case of Guru Nanak tributes have been paid by many people who are not Sikhs. In north India there is a rhyme:

Baba Nanak Shah Fakir
Hindu ka Guru Musulman ka Pir

This means that Nanak was highly respected for his goodness and that the Hindus looked on him as a teacher while the Muslims called him a saint.

An extremely distinguished Muslim poet, Sir Mohammad Iqbal (1877-1938), composed a poem called 'Nanak'. He wrote it in Urdu, the language which is now the official language of Pakistan, and he started it by comparing Guru Nanak to the Buddha, the 'founder' of another great religion, and ended it with words that praised Guru Nanak's vision of the unity of God.

It is easy to see how Guru Nanak's influence carries on in different parts of the world today. For instance, in Birmingham, Bristol, Coventry, Dudley, Glasgow, Hitchin, Huddersfield, Leicester, Leeds, Nottingham, Preston, Rugby, Smethwick, Stoke-on-Trent, Wolverhampton and other places in Britain you may see *gurdwaras* (Sikh places of worship) that have been called after him. Worldwide there are many, many more. The reproduction on this page is from a leaflet produced by a Gurdwara, named after Guru Nanak, in Singapore.

In his autobiography a Canadian Sikh, Tara Singh Bains, provides illustrations of Guru Nanak's continuing influence: he recalls how, like thousands of other Sikhs, his father told him to memorise the morning prayer that Guru Nanak had composed.

> It has thirty-eight verses and takes twenty minutes to recite. It was the only verse from the holy scriptures that I learned by heart before I became an independent person. Father made me do it...but it was a good thing.

Tara Singh Bains goes on to describe how he stopped being afraid of dying because 'one night I saw Guru Nanak in my dream.'

Why should a person who died more than four and a half centuries ago still have so much influence on people living not only in India but also in Britain, Canada and other parts of the world?

Leaflet from Gurdwara Katong, Singapore.

12

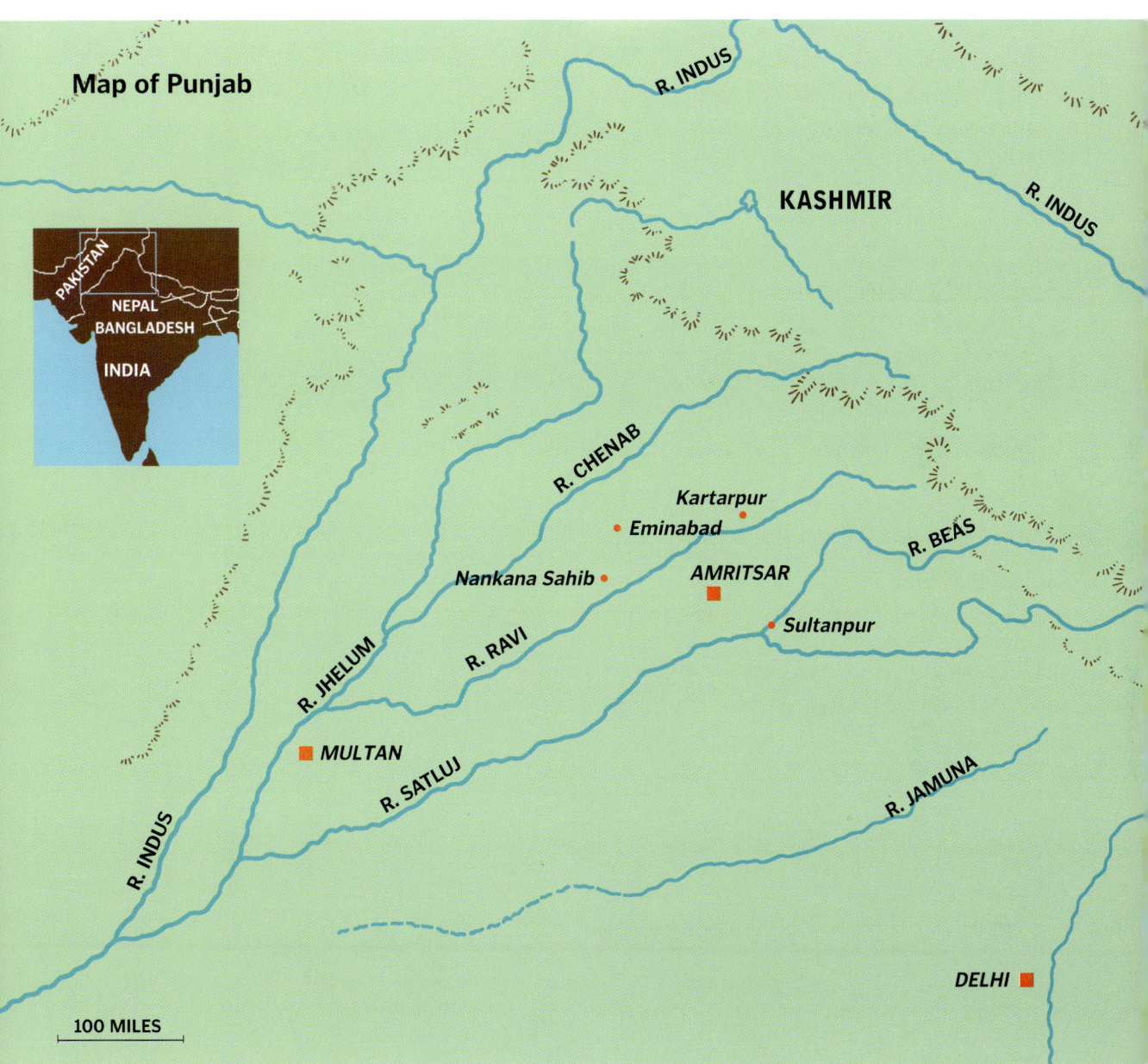

Guru Nanak as a boy with Rai Bular and the angry farmer.
(see opposite)

Here are two of the stories about Guru Nanak's early life which Sikh parents tell their children.

1) One day the young Guru Nanak took the buffaloes to graze and fell asleep at the edge of a wheatfield. While he was asleep the buffaloes trampled all over the field eating the wheat. The owner of the crop appeared and was furious when he found that his harvest had been ruined. He became even angrier when Nanak said, 'Nothing of yours has been damaged,' and complained to Rai Bular, the village landlord. Guru Nanak's father was summoned and told to reprimand his son and pay for the damage. At this point Nanak repeated, 'Nothing has been damaged, not even a blade of grass. Send someone to see.' Rai Bular sent his messenger, who returned, saying in astonishment, 'Indeed, nothing has been harmed.'

2) While he was still a child Nanak went out one morning and lay down to rest under a shady tree. He fell asleep and remained there all day without changing his position, although of course the angle of the sunlight changed as the hours passed. Rai Bular was going hunting and happened to pass the tree. To his amazement he noticed that whereas all the other trees' shadows had moved the shadow of this tree had remained stationary. He ordered his companions to wake the sleeping boy so that they could find out who he was. On discovering that it was Mehta Kalu's son, Nanak, who was protected from the heat in this miraculous way, Rai Bular was convinced that Nanak was someone especially blessed by God.

Of course, miracle stories tend to be told about exceptional people, even those who have lived relatively recently. In order to understand why Guru Nanak is still so influential we need to examine what is reported about Guru Nanak's life in more detail and to listen to his teaching. Just as you can summarise your life in a c.v., so we can write down the information which we have about Guru Nanak's life in the form of a brief *curriculum vitae*.

Guru Nanak

Birth: 1469 in Rai Bhoi di Talvandi, Punjab (now in Pakistan), to Mehta Kalu and Tripta
Education: school in Rai Bhoi di Talvandi
Marriage: to Sulakhani
Children: two sons - Lakhmi Das and Siri Chand
Employment: storekeeper (for Daulat Khan Lodi in Sultanpur); preacher (for God)
Travel: very extensive (including Mecca and Baghdad)
Organisation: a new community of followers in a new village, Kartarpur (in Punjab, Pakistan)
Compositions: 974 hymns in the Guru Granth Sahib
Death: 1539 in Kartarpur

All over the world Sikhs and very many others respect the teachings of the *Guru Granth Sahib*. This is not just a treasured book but is regarded by Sikhs as a living Guru in the sense of embodying the Guru's divine powers. Guru Nanak's 974 hymns make up a large part of its text. Like other popular teachers at that time, Guru Nanak sang his ideas to music and used poetry not prose. Translations are never the same as the original, and poetry is particularly difficult to translate in a way which is accurate and still as moving and memorable as the poet's actual words. These verses will give you a hint of his message.

> If like a bird I could heavenward soar,
>   with a hundred such realms in my reach;
> And change so that no-one might see me
>   and live with no food and no drink,
> Yet would your glory transcend all my striving -
>   no words can encompass the Name.
>
> If I could read with the eye of intelligence
>   paper of infinite weight;
> If I could write with the winds everlasting,
>   and pens dipped in oceans of ink,
> Yet would your glory transcend all my striving -
>   no words can encompass the Name.

You will notice that Guru Nanak constantly mentions the Name (in Punjabi **Nam** which rhymes with 'palm'), meaning the name—in fact the reality—of God. In this book you will find both the Punjabi word *Nam* and the English word Name (always with a capital letter when it is translating *Nam*).

You may be wondering why the word *Nam* is so similar to 'name' in English. No, it's not because Indian languages have absorbed words from English. If you look at the word for name in lots of different European languages and Indian languages you will find a similar word (*nom* in French and *nome* in Italian). This is because these languages all belong to one family which includes ancient languages such as Sanskrit and Latin as well as more recent ones that are spoken today. Over the centuries languages have changed, but some words still remain as evidence of this close relationship. The language that Guru Nanak used is like a distant relative to English.

In the next chapter we will think about whether we can ever know what famous people were really like and what really happened in their lives.

Guru Nanak leaving his home and family and setting out to preach his message. This undated picture was discovered in the late twentieth century at the site of the Bebe Nanaki Gurdwara in Sultanpur, Punjab. Bebe Nanaki was Guru Nanak's sister. Many accounts talk of her great insight and devotion, and she is often regarded by Sikhs as the Guru's first disciple.

Chapter 2: Can we really know what famous people were like?

From chapter 1 you will already have a picture in your mind of Guru Nanak. What does he look like? Probably a venerable old man with a long white beard, a kindly expression and with one hand raised in blessing.

If you go to Sikh homes or places of worship you are bound to notice Guru Nanak's picture. Sometimes this is framed, sometimes it is part of a trade calendar for that year and so advertises the business of the shopkeeper who had copies printed for his customers. Very often the picture is a reproduction of a painting by the celebrated Sikh artist, Sobha Singh. Even if it is just an unframed calendar picture Sikhs will treat it with respect - they wouldn't put it on the floor for example.

But is this really what Guru Nanak looked like? Obviously there were no cameras around in 1500, and although court painters produced portraits of the emperors who ruled India at the time there is no known portrait of Guru Nanak 'from life'.

Pencil drawing of Guru Nanak by Harpal Singh (1994)

Can we say with certainty what Guru Nanak looked like? The Canadian, Tara Singh, is critical of Sikhs who seem to worship pictures of Guru Nanak:

> Some innocent Sikhs bow their heads before pictures of the Sikh Gurus... these pictures only represent the calibre of the artist...

What he means is that a painting by, say, Sobha Singh, tells us more about his convictions and perceptions and his skill as a painter than about Guru Nanak himself.

This is a popular image of Guru Nanak by Bhagat Singh, who painted in India in the twentieth century. Notice the ways in which the artist shows that he was a traveller and that he was a man of prayer.

But a picture can also communicate a vision which has had a deep impact on the artist's mind. Religious people from all faiths have dreams and visions in which saints and spiritual teachers, including those who lived centuries earlier, appear to them. As you've just read, a Canadian Sikh, Tara Singh, saw Guru Nanak in his dreams. Can you spot any differences between the oldest pictures of Guru Nanak and the more recent ones? You may notice that in recent paintings he always wears a turban, but in older pictures he has a different sort of head covering, more like a crown in shape. Can you think why this change has occurred? You will need to look at the influence of Guru Nanak's ninth successor as Guru, Guru Gobind Singh, on the rules for committed Sikhs' appearance.

You may also be wondering whether pictures—even photographs—are necessarily the best way of knowing what someone was like as a person. What about the things that have been written about them?

The *Guru Granth Sahib* does not contain accounts of people's lives. For episodes in the life of Guru Nanak, we need to turn to collections of stories known as **janam sakhis**.

Most Sikhs hear the stories, like those retold in chapter 1, from their relatives. In the past at least, grandparents used to find time to tell their grandchildren religious stories. You can also hear them from preachers and singers in the *gurdwara*. But there are written versions as well. Collections of *janam sakhi* stories in Punjabi, English and other languages have been published for children. These are based on older versions. The reading list at the end of this book provides information about these.

In 1733 a scribe (a man whose profession was writing things down for other people) called Daya Ram wrote a life story or *janam sakhi* of Guru Nanak. Each episode is written in Punjabi and many are illustrated with colourful pictures. These scenes from Guru Nanak's life were painted in bright colours by an artist called Alam Chand Raj. (The name Raj indicates that he was also a mason.) The manuscript is one of many that tell Guru Nanak's life story. Several of these manuscripts are stored in London in the India Office Library. In a library every book (or manuscript) has its own separate number. This is called its accession number and it is used to identify each of the hundreds of thousands of items that are stored in the library. Daya Ram's manuscript has the accession number B40, and so it is known as the B40 *janam sakhi*.

From the narrative and the illustrations in the B40 and other *janam sakhis* we can form some impression of Guru Nanak. But they were written two or three hundred years after his death. Some of these stories describe extraordinary miracles. Why should this be when Guru Nanak (and his successors) seem to have criticised miracle-workers? It is not that the Gurus denied the possibility of miraculous feats; instead, they preferred to put emphasis on straightforward

B40 *Janam Sakhi* painting showing four pennants and the wealthy Duni Chand begging for forgiveness. Guru Nanak is accompanied by Bhai Mardana (17th century).

acts of kindness to others, and urged people to recognise life itself as a miracle worthy of wonder. The *janam sakhis* which Sikhs tell most often are ones which make points that are in keeping with the message of Guru Nanak's hymns. The example that follows is based on the narrative in the B40 *janam sakhi*:

> During his extensive travels Guru Nanak came to a town in which four pennants caught his eye. When he enquired from the locals what these flags meant they told him that a rich money-lender (Duni Chand by name in some versions of the story) was flying them above his four chests full of treasure. So Guru Nanak went to the money-lender and respectfully asked him why he had set up the pennants. The money-lender explained that when he died these pennants would go with him. The Guru then gave him a needle and requested him to keep it safe for him until they met up in heaven. After a while the money-lender began worrying about how he could do what Guru Nanak had asked of him and he ran after him to beg him to take his needle back as there was no point in his keeping it. Guru Nanak's response was to ask him how he thought his money chests could go with him into the afterlife. At this point the money-lender saw how foolish he had been. He begged the Guru to forgive him, then went home, gave all his property away and happily devoted his life to following the Guru's rule for a wholesome life: repeating God's name, giving to others and regular bathing.

But first a word of caution, based on the experience of another faith, Christianity. Jesus lived two thousand years ago and his life has influenced millions of people. But if you look at the four accounts of his life, the Gospels in the New Testament (the second major section of the Bible) you will notice that there are all sorts of differences between the four accounts.

This is not surprising, as the Gospels were not written until some years after Jesus had died, and they were written by people who had strong convictions about Jesus's meaning for the world. There were no reporters following Jesus around and there was no television or radio. Scholars continue to search for what Jesus was really like, 'the historical Jesus'. However, the fact that there are tantalising differences between the Gospel stories and that so much remains a mystery doesn't weaken Christians' convictions about Jesus's message of love or their faith that death was not the end of him.

Or we can think of much more recent events too. Have you noticed how different witnesses' memories of what happened—perhaps a music festival or a railway accident—are sometimes significantly different? Does this disprove that the event took place or mean that the witnesses are lying?

Even in the case of celebrities who are widely reported in the media, there are different—sometimes violently opposed—assessments of their characters and achievements. Before her tragic death in a car crash in 1997 people who knew Princess Diana expressed a variety of opinions about the things she did and why she did them. After her death newspapers published different explanations for the fatal accident.

Do you think it is possible to know what happened in the past or what a person was like? Does this matter?

Guru Nanak lived about five hundred years ago and many of his followers have a clear idea of his message and his importance to the world. What we can definitely do is build up our own impressions based on what he said and not just what others have said about him. And for this we can turn to the *Guru Granth Sahib*, which contains many of his compositions.

He probably didn't sit down and write out these verses as the ideas came to him. Instead it is said that he experienced 'the **bani** [the divine word] descending', and immediately sang his compositions. Guru Nanak's companion was a Muslim musician called Mardana and he played the melodies for him on his guitar-like **rabab**. Imagine a crowd gathering around them and joining in the singing and memorising the words. Even if the words were written down some time later there is no reason why they should have changed. We know that the hymns were part of a collection which was copied out by the grandson of the third Guru (Amar Das) who became Guru thirteen years after Guru Nanak's death. These manuscripts are known as the **Mohan Pothis**. *Pothi* means a book and Mohan was the name of Guru Amar Das's son. (To pronounce '*pothi*' correctly try making it rhyme with 'note he'.) When the fifth Guru, Arjan Dev, compiled the first volume of Sikh scripture (the Adi Granth), he included Guru Nanak's hymns from the *Mohan Pothis*.

Poems are like letters. The writers are keen to communicate their ideas, and the way they do this gives a glimpse of their own personalities and interests. Look again at the translation of one of Guru Nanak's poems at the end of chapter 1. What is a person who writes like this interested in? Guru Nanak's poems are all about how humans actually live their lives (usually out of touch with God) and how they should live in order to be in tune with God's will for the world. To make his point more memorably, the poems are like snapshots in words. We get flashes of changing seasons in the Punjab countryside and details of the lives of farmers, businessmen and others. The hymns mention birds, fish and trees and people of different religions— Hindu and Muslim—worshipping God in their distinctive ways. (The next chapter gives some examples.) He composed poems in different metres to be sung to tunes which make anyone who is listening feel a sense of peace or a longing to follow God's will, or to wonder at the marvels of nature.

All this tells us that Guru Nanak was observant, sensitive and creative and that he was extremely single-minded. He was keen to help others to transform their lives, and so he used the most persuasive language he could. He did not use the ancient language of Sanskrit which the Hindu priests chanted but which ordinary folk could not understand. Instead he used words which made immediate sense to his hearers. The fact that his poems were remembered, treasured and included in a sacred book shows that his followers felt deeply that his message really could transform people's lives.

You will remember from the end of chapter 1 that *Nam* means more than 'name', so repeating God's name involves concentrating on the real nature of God.

Guru Nanak with Bhai Mardana (playing *rabab*) and Bhai Bala, waving peacock fan.

Chapter 3: Does life have a meaning?

Have you worked out what the meaning of life is? To put this another way - what is the purpose of our human life? Or what is the most important thing in life—or at least in your life?

The Big Issue is a magazine which is sold by homeless people and the profits help them to pay for somewhere to live. This poem (by D-) appeared in one issue:

> At times like these
> I could wish for anything
> Everything
>
> Like whiter teeth
> A straighter nose
> To see without the use of lenses
> And a bank account
> full to bursting with clean crisp cash.
>
> Or that piece of land
> With the chicken, the goats,
> And maybe even a sheep or two.
> Bricks and mortar, boards and plaster
> Furniture, furnishings and fripperies...
> Plus a healthy smattering of
> Equatorial sunshine...
>
> Gifts,
> Talent,
> Inner serenity,
> And a big red and black
> Polka-dot fun-fur coat...

What might your wish-poem include?

Or we can look at life in another way. We recognise that there are natural 'laws' or patterns that

A woman reading the *Guru Granth Sahib*. Notice the *chauri (see chapter 11)*.

we can predict and rely on. We know for example that apples fall to the ground because of gravity and that the sun rises once a day. But are there other laws and patterns which help us to lead happy, useful lives?

Guru Nanak's poems show how he had decoded the confusing world that we inhabit. He spent many years travelling to share his answers to life's riddles with as many people as possible. You will find these in the chapters that follow: the essence of these is that humans need to reorientate their lives, abandoning any false sense of their own ego and instead concentrating on God and serving other people, as the Guru directs us.

You may wonder how Guru Nanak had so much conviction—what happened to change his life from working each day as a store-keeper for Daulat Khan to travelling long distances to try to encourage people to live in a more meaningful way.

According to the B40 *janam sakhi* Guru Nanak used to go to bathe in the nearby river Vein (or Bein) every day. One day his servant returned alone to the Khan to tell him that Guru Nanak had gone into the water but had failed to reappear. The Khan was very upset and ordered boatmen to drag the river with their nets. Obviously he assumed that his employee had drowned but, to everyone's surprise, Guru Nanak emerged again after three days. Almost more surprisingly he went straight home and, without uttering a word, he gave away all his possessions. For several days he would wear almost no clothes and he remained absolutely silent. When eventually he began to speak again he said:

> There is neither Hindu nor Muslim.

When he was asked to explain what he meant he composed a short poem in which he suggests the qualities that a true Muslim would have such as compassion. On another occasion he expressed similar insights, but this time he used the image of a Hindu ascetic, a **yogi**.

From now on he acted with a strong sense of purpose and taught anyone who would listen to him about the real meaning of life.

Probably one of the first things that Guru Nanak did after this experience in the river Vein was to compose the **Japji*** ('jap' rhymes with 'cup'). This sets out his discoveries about the meaning of life. The title means that it is a poem which needs to be repeated and remembered. (In Punjabi *jap* means 'repeat something over and over again while you reflect on it' and '*ji*' is a way of saying that you respect something or someone.) You will recall that the Canadian, Tara Singh, was glad that his father had told him to recite the *Japji* every day.

Just to give one more example of the impact of reciting *Japji* on ordinary individuals' lives, Bhai Randhir Singh, who lived from 1879 to 1961, became a freedom-fighter —a brave man who suffered years of harsh imprisonment. This was because he was struggling to free India from being governed by the British as part of the Empire. As a young man Bhai Randhir Singh, like Guru Nanak, had had a powerful experience which changed his whole life, making him ready to sacrifice everything for his principles. This change came about as a result of reading the *Japji* each morning —something his father had told him to do if he wanted to pass his examinations that year!

*   *Japji* is usually called *Japji Sahib*. *Sahib* is a term showing respect, as in the title of the *Guru Granth Sahib*.

Amrit and Rabindra Kaur Singh are twin Sikh artists from Britain. This painting by Rabindra Kaur shows Guru Nanak's enlightenment as they imagine it. Notice how they use techniques from much older Indian miniature painting, and also how the artists' imagination provides details that are not given in the *janam sakhi* account.

According to the *Japji* it is God's will or 'divine order' which is the most important fact about the universe. The word that Guru Nanak used for this 'will' was **hukam**. Everything has been created as it is in accordance with God's *hukam*. If human beings are to lead happy, compassionate lives they must be in tune with this *hukam*, not kicking against it. This is because, when Guru Nanak used the word *hukam* he meant not just a physical principle, like the law of gravity, but also a moral principle. You may have heard statements like 'What goes around comes around' or 'We reap what we sow'. If we act according to what we know of God's plan or pattern then we are rewarded. The reward is being in harmony with God.

Another important word in the *Japji* is *Nam*. Look at the Glossary if you are still unsure of its meaning. In fact the English word name doesn't help us very much in understanding what Guru Nanak meant. For him *Nam* is a word for the whole truth about God - not just God's name. This is why we have given it a capital letter. Guru Nanak says that if we concentrate our minds on this truth, rather than on all the things that usually attract our attention (like the 'polka-dot fun-fur coat' in *The Big Issue* poem), we will feel deep peace.

But what is God like? The opening words of the *Japji* are:

> There is One Being
> Truth by Name
> Creator
> Without fear
> Without hatred
> Timeless in form
> Unborn
> Self-existent
> The grace of the Guru.

In Punjabi this is called the **Mul Mantar** (also written in English as Mool Mantra). The *Mul Mantar* is rather like a telegram. When people had to send urgent messages by telegram they had to pay a certain amount per word, so the secret was to say as much as you could, as clearly as you could, in as few words as possible.

If you had to convey your ideas and beliefs about God or about the meaning of life in not more than 25 words, what would you say? In fact, in the original language, Guru Nanak used just twelve words plus a numeral (1).

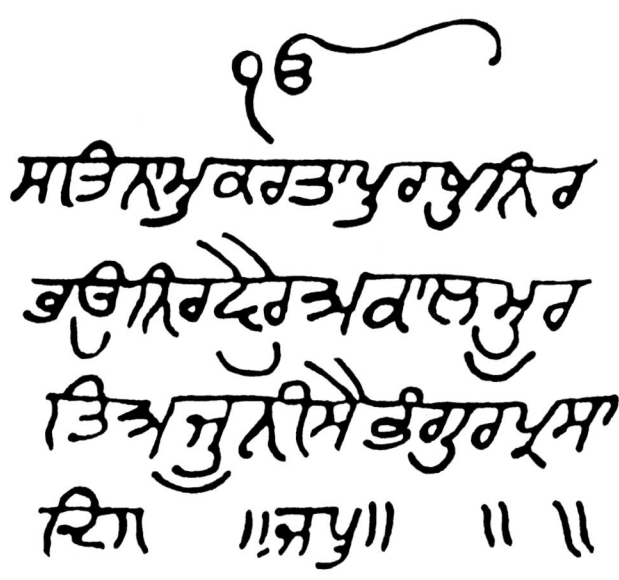

Mul Mantar believed to be in handwriting of the fifth Guru, Guru Arjan Dev, or at least dictated by him, from a text of the scriptures kept in the Punjabi town of Kartarpur and so known as the *Kartarpuri Bir* (volume).

After this very concise introduction, Guru Nanak composed 38 verses about how we should live and the last words of the *Japji* give this summary:

> Air is our Guru, water our father,
> and the great earth our mother.
> Day and night are the female and male nurses
> in whose laps the whole universe plays.
> Good and bad deeds are all disclosed
> in the presence of Righteousness.
> Our actions take us near or far.
> Those who remember the Name earn true success.
> Nanak says their faces shine,
> and they take many with them to liberation.

Liberation refers to the belief that we are born many many times until (as a result of doing good) we are free to be with God and do not have to be born all over again. What do you think happens to us after we die?

Guru Nanak in a forest (*The Pool of Immortality* by Amrit and Rabindra Kaur Singh).

Chapter 4: Can our specific experiences teach us universal truths?

Think global, act local
Have you ever heard of this phrase? It was used by a well known charity, in its campaign to encourage us to live in an environmentally friendly way, within our families, communities and towns, so that we could contribute to the greater good of the world. Another way of understanding the distinction between local and global is to think of the specific details of our own lives as microcosms (miniature versions) of what is true on a world-wide scale.

As we have seen, Guru Nanak has been praised by people from many walks of life for the universal values of humanity and spiritual sincerity which he encouraged us to live by. In this way, his message goes beyond all social and cultural barriers. However, he is also associated closely with his homeland, the Punjab. It was here that he returned—after making his four journeys to the east, west, north and south—and here he established a community of Sikhs.

Indeed, Guru Nanak's **shabads** (hymns) show a distinct sense of 'presence' or 'here-ness' in the world. He glimpsed the divine through his everyday surroundings and activities which provided clues for his vision of how one ought to live. Here is an example:

> If my body were a vat and the crimson of the Name
> Were poured into it,
> And if the dyer were my Lord
> Such a brilliant colour you would never have seen!

(Remember, before the days of mass-production, the job of the dyer literally lent colour to people's lives!)

And again:

> Make your mind the plough and your deeds the farming,
> Let your body be the field and steady work the watering.
> Let the Divine Name be the seed you plant.
> Cover it safely with the tools of contentment
> And let humility be the fence that protects it.
> Through tending it with love the seed will sprout,
> And fortunate will then be your home.

Guru Nanak ploughing by Anil Sharma

Note the ways in which Guru Nanak is drawing a series of comparisons between farming and nurturing a life of meditation on God. He actually uses agricultural terms as a way of speaking about this cultivation of spirituality. Look at the picture above and decide whether, by painting Guru Nanak actually ploughing a field, the artist has missed the point that Guru Nanak was expressing, or whether such a picture helps people to reflect on the deeper meaning of the Guru's picture language.

And so we come across the lives of farmers, craftsmen, traders, holy men, and women and others in various roles who made up the social fabric of Guru Nanak's Punjab. See which of these you can find elsewhere in this book. Whatever their occupation, he would teach by referring to experiences familiar to them and so 'speak their language' to convey a message.

We also picture natural surroundings as we hear Guru Nanak's compositions—the changing seasons, rivers, sea and mountains, birds and animals. Their role is never just to set a beautiful scene; always their inclusion will jolt us into a deeper awareness.

> You are like the ocean, seeing and knowing everything;
> I am a fish - how can I measure you?
> Wherever I turn, it is you I find.
> The moment I get away, I die.

All of us have had experiences which, sometimes quite strikingly, throw light on what we might see as a 'universal truth'. Pause for a few moments to ask yourself what we mean when we call something a 'universal truth'. These enlightening experiences might be as momentous as climbing to the top of a mountain, realising that patience and persistence will help you reach your goal. It might be as simple as biting into a shiny red apple to find it tasteless, a reminder that appearances can be deceptive, and all that glitters is not gold! Cultures the world over have sayings like this where something specific points to a universally held fact or belief. When we hear them we can nod with instant recognition.

Two Sikh boys in the Punjab countryside. It was the Punjab landscape which inspired much of Guru Nanak's poetry.

It is precisely this nod, this moment of understanding, which Guru Nanak aimed to trigger in his listeners by basing his teaching on concrete, 'worldly' experiences. His approach was not to lay down rules and abstract theories, or to dismiss our everyday lives or responsibilities and dwell only on another world or afterlife. Rather, his verses reveal that he was connected to the here and now, whilst rising above it, and he encouraged his followers to do likewise.

For many people, Sikhs included, the Sikh religion seems to pose a paradox. How can a faith founded on principles so universal still have an identity that seems so separate and distinct? We will discuss this further in Chapter 6.

For the moment, however, you might like to consider the implications for you of the motto, 'Think global, act local', and discuss ways in which a universal principle can be found in something which at first glance can seem limited and specific. Given Guru Nanak's specific culture, language, and historic era, what shows us that his awareness went beyond such barriers?

Chapter 5: How do we communicate most effectively what matters most?

Today there are more ways of communicating with other people than ever before. But not everyone has access to every means of communicating, and different sorts of information may need to be relayed in different ways.

To start with language: English is more widely understood than Finnish or Rumanian, but that doesn't mean that everyone understands English. Turning to the method of communication—many people in the world cannot read or write, and many millions more have no access to a modem or a computer.

Now think about the information which you have remembered longest and most easily. It is likely to include rhymes, especially ones with a catchy tune. You probably find some eye-catching images easy to remember too, like logos and famous brand names. Think about an advertisement that works well. Why does it catch your attention and remain in your memory?

Some messages are extremely important—they may even be matters of life or death. How you send the information makes all the difference. If the house is on fire you probably won't start e-mailing people to rescue you. If you are in love you might send a rose or a valentine or a long letter.

This brings us back to Guru Nanak. Ever since his experience in the river Vein he knew he had been called by God to make a dramatic change to other people's lives. If you had been living at that time, how would you have tried to reach as many people as effectively as possible? From previous chapters you already know some of the ways in which he set about passing on his message.

Travel

First, Guru Nanak travelled extensively and often in difficult conditions. According to the *janam sakhis* he went as far as Baghdad (Iraq) and Mecca (in Saudi Arabia) in the west, as far as Sri Lanka in the south, to a mountainous region (probably Tibet) in the north and into the far east of India (Assam). Through his journeys he encountered different kinds of people along the way, and shared his insights and broad vision in a variety of situations. Many of these are documented in the *janam sakhis* and there are hints of these in his hymns.

Jaswant Singh's painting suggests Guru Nanak striding over the world to spread his message.

Language

Second, he spoke in words that people understood. That may seem an obvious thing to do, but Hindus and Muslims in India—like members of other faiths for centuries—were used to hearing religious information, such as verses from their holy books, in Sanskrit and Arabic respectively. Only unusually learned individuals (such as Hindu priests from the **Brahmin** caste) actually understood the full meaning of the words. The language which Guru Nanak used is less familiar today, but it is very similar to the modern languages of Punjabi and Hindi. It includes words from other languages too. For instance the names which he used for God come from Arabic, Persian and Sanskrit. In this way the language made connections with hearers from different religious communities.

Yes, 'hearers': most of the people whom Guru Nanak met did not need to read or write, unless

Picture of Guru Nanak and Mardana with Muslim pilgrims passing by (from B40 *janam sakhi*).

they were accountants (like his relatives from the *Khatri* caste) or priests. As you read in chapter 1, he sang his message to a musical accompaniment, and he used poetry rather than prose. These are efficient ways of communicating too.

Music

If you study classical Indian music you discover that different combinations of notes affect your mood in different ways. Some melodies make you feel sad, and if you are happy you prefer different music from when you are upset. This is not peculiar to Indian music of course. Why is music played in supermarkets and restaurants? What sorts of music would you be unlikely to hear there? Why did the Turkish authorities in 1998 decide to play soothing Western classical music to calm their riot police as they waited behind the scenes in their coaches? Why do you think that the Greek philosopher Plato (nearly 2,500 years ago) decided that music could have a harmful influence on people and should be banned from an ideal society?

Raga is the word for the combinations of notes on which Indian music is based, and each *raga* has its own distinctive name such as Asa, Ramkali and Sri. In Punjabi this word is **rag,** pronounced raag, i.e. rhyming with the first syllable of Margaret. Guru Nanak used 31 *rags*. Their purpose was not just to decorate or embellish what he had to say. Rather, setting words to *rags* allowed for a richer, more resonant and memorable expression of what Guru Nanak thought and felt.

Has it ever occurred to you that the *way* something is said is often just as important as what is said itself? This could be a declaration of love or a firm reprimand. The manner of communication can affect us just as much as the thing being communicated. Music helps create what you could call an 'emotive meaning', which allows us to grasp the Guru's message more fully, by evoking a sense of wonder, or of yearning for God, inspiring us to action, or humbling us to realise our shortcomings.

By singing these hymns and listening to them Guru Nanak's followers could bring themselves into tune with God's will. Have you noticed too how when we sing we can go beyond what our inhibitions allow us to say?

The English Patient is a famous film based on a novel by Michael Ondaatje. One of the principal characters (who plays a more important role in the book than in the film) is a Sikh sapper called Kirpal Singh or Kip for short whose speciality is defusing mines. At one point he recalls the beauty and importance of music in Sikh worship:

> If I took you before morning you would see first of all the mist over the water. Then it lifts to reveal the temple in light. You will already be hearing the hymns of the saints—Ramanand, Nanak and Kabir. Singing is at the centre of worship...The temple is a haven in the flux of life, accessible to all.

Kip is remembering the Golden Temple (Harmandir Sahib) in Amritsar, Punjab. But Guru Nanak's hymns (his **shabads**) are sung like this in every *gurdwara*. These days the musical instruments most commonly used are the *tabla* (drums) and *vaja* (harmonium) as shown in the picture below, although as you can see from other illustrations in the book, Guru Nanak was accompanied by a stringed instrument called the *rabab*, which was played by his companion, Mardana.

Sikhs performing *kirtan* (singing of *shabads*/hymns) in a London gurdwara. The Punjabi words come from a popular verse celebrating Guru Nanak's birth, saying that it brought light into a gloomy world.

Logo

Guru Nanak's strongest conviction was that there is one God, or to put it another way: the basic, underlying reality in the world - what is most real - is a unity. His statement of belief comes right at the beginning of the *Guru Granth Sahib* and begins with ੴ. This consists of the digit for 1 from the Punjabi number system and the **oankar** which relates to the sacred syllable **om** (pronounced to rhyme with 'home')*. This syllable (ॐ in Sanskrit) had been used by Hindus for centuries as a way of representing God in sound. Try chanting 'om' by breathing in deeply and then exhaling very, very slowly. As you breathe out chant (for as long as you can hold it) 'ah', then 'oo' and finally, 'mm', all in one deep breath, until there is no more breath in your lungs. This long vibrating sound has for centuries in India been an image of God in sound.

Why do you think that Guru Nanak chose this way - a numeral and a sacred sound - to make his point? One answer is that the *word* 'one' (*ik* in Punjabi) actually consists of several letters, whereas the *number* is indivisible.

But *om* and *ik oankar* are also striking symbols on paper. ੴ is an excellent logo for the Sikh faith. If you see someone wearing a ring with this sign on it you know that the wearer is likely to be a Sikh. See how many times you can spot ੴ in this book.

Acted Signs

Think back to the story of the pennants in chapter 2. How did Guru Nanak make his point? From this and other stories you will notice that he had another very effective method of communicating as well. Even if everything in the *janam sakhis* did not happen exactly as reported, it seems likely that he also acted out signs. Effective teachers (including Jesus and some of the Jewish prophets) have often made their point dramatically. Of course many of their followers remember these acted signs as being miraculous events—feats that no ordinary person could perform. To understand fully the story which follows you need to bear in mind that traditionally society in India is divided into castes. Five hundred years ago this system was more rigid than nowadays. Members of some castes would have far more power and influence than members of others: which caste a person belongs to is decided by being born into a family of a particular

---

* The Punjabi numeral ੧ is related to the 1 which we use. This is because 'Arabic' number system, which travelling Arab traders introduced to Europe, was a version of the older systems that had already been in use in India for many centuries.

caste. You also need to know that Hindus may carry on showing respect to their forbears long after they have died. The ceremonies that they perform to obtain blessings for their ancestors involve honouring members of the *Brahmin* caste (hereditary priests) with gifts and food. Cows, regarded as mothers (or symbolising motherhood) because they feed us with their milk, were a traditional gift. Here is the story:

> News spread around the village of Eminabad that Guru Nanak, a saintly person, was staying at the house of a carpenter named Lalo. [Carpenters belong to a caste that is often looked down on by people of higher caste.] A much wealthier resident, Malak Bhago, a revenue collector, who like Guru Nanak belonged to the *Khatri* caste, was hosting an impressive religious occasion for the benefit of his ancestors. This event involved presenting a very large number of *Brahmins* with cows. He insisted that Guru Nanak should come to his house to share the feast he had prepared for the *Brahmins*. When the Guru arrived he put sumptuous food in front of him and asked why such a distinguished holy man had been eating with a low caste carpenter rather than with *Khatris* and *Brahmins*. The Guru's response was to ask someone to fetch from Lalo's house the food that he had been eating there. When this was brought to him he held it in one hand and one of the revenue collector's *puris* [deep fried *chapatis*] in the other and squeezed. Milk dripped out of Lalo's food while blood oozed from the *puri*. Guru Nanak explained that Lalo's food had been earned honestly whereas Bhago was trying to honour his ancestors with what had in effect been stolen from others. He ordered him to pay for the cows which he had seized before making his offering to the *Brahmins*.

Many pictures show Guru Nanak's acted sign, the squeezing of his two hosts' food to emphasise his teaching. This next one, less usually, shows Guru Nanak blessing Bhai Lalo by his work bench.

Challenging questions

Guru Nanak used teasing questions as well to make people think. Can you remember the example of this in the story of the rich man and the needle?

To sum up, Guru Nanak communicated his message by travelling extensively, speaking a familiar language and singing his message as poems accompanied by inspiring music. He stated the most important truth about God briefly and forcefully. When this is written down it becomes a logo, a sacred symbol, which often appears on pictures, calendars, badges or rings. He also acted out his teaching dramatically.

Guru Nanak visits Bhai Lalo, the carpenter.

Chapter 6: Are labels and uniforms necessary?

In this chapter we will look at what Guru Nanak thought of religious labels, at what the label 'Sikh' means and whether there is any value in members of groups being identifiable, particularly by what they wear. Before turning our attention to Guru Nanak here is a story set in Northern Ireland from a book by Anthony de Mello entitled *Awareness*. Does this story anger you, offend you, make you want to laugh or protest?

"Well, somebody told me another story, about Paddy. Paddy was walking down the street in Belfast and he discovers a gun pressing against the back of his head and a voice says, 'Are you Catholic or Protestant?' Well, Paddy has to do some pretty fast thinking. He says, 'I'm a Jew.' And he hears a voice say, 'I've got to be the luckiest Arab in the whole of Belfast.'"

What point is Anthony de Mello trying to make by telling this grim joke? And what is the connection with Guru Nanak?

Look back at chapter 3 to the Guru's first words after his transforming experience in the river. 'There is no Hindu; there is no Muslim.' Just as in Northern Ireland today the majority of people are either Protestant or Catholic, so in Guru Nanak's context almost everyone was either a Muslim or a Hindu.

Selling Sikh badges and symbols in the gurdwara.

One way of understanding this riddle is that very few people are true Hindus or Muslims, as very few really live up to the highest principles of their faith.

But another interpretation (or way of understanding the meaning) is that labels—especially religious labels—are actually unhelpful. They divide up the human family unnecessarily, often with disastrous and evil consequences like wars. In the name of religion someone may kill a complete stranger just because that individual can be identified as a member of a different group—a Muslim, a Jew or a Communist for example.

Guru Nanak and the Gurus who succeeded him encouraged their followers to adopt a way of life which ignored old labels. Some pictures show Guru Nanak seated between two faithful companions, Bhai Bala, a Hindu, and Bhai Mardana, a Muslim musician. The language which he used in his hymns includes both Muslim and Hindu ways of referring to God—as Allah (the Arabic word), Khudai (a Persian word), and as Hari and Ram (two words that Hindus were comfortable with).

Janam sakhi stories describe Guru Nanak visiting the holy sites of both communities, both Mecca and the banks of the Hindus' sacred river Ganges—perhaps at the famous pilgrimage place of Hardwar. Another story concerns his death. Muslims and Hindus were arguing over his dead body, as each group claimed that the Guru belonged to their community. Muslims are buried when they die whereas Hindus are cremated, so the Muslims wanted to bury his body and the Hindus to put it on a funeral pyre. According to tradition the Guru's body disappeared and flowers appeared in its place. What point is this story making?

Chapter 5 included a quotation from *The English Patient*. If you read the book or see the film you realise that the 'English patient' is not English, but that during the Second World War people's death or survival depended on how others labelled them—according to language or country of origin.

What religious labels do you know? Some, like Buddhist, Christian, Hindu and Muslim belong to hundreds of millions of people. All these faith traditions consist of many smaller groups, each with its own name: Baptist, Brethren, Catholic, Jehovah's Witness, Jesus' Army, Mormon, Namdhari, Orthodox, Protestant, Reform, Swaminarayan. Notice whether you react to any of these and, if so, ask yourself what picture comes to mind and whether you have any positive or negative feelings about this group of people.

The label 'Christian' began as a nickname for people who believed in Jesus as Christ. (*Christos* is the Greek word for 'messiah' or 'anointed one'.) The label 'Hindu' was given to the inhabitants of India by Persians and other people who came from countries further west. (The word 'Hindu' is derived from the name of the river Indus which is 'Sindhu' in Sanskrit.) The name for the followers of Guru Nanak and his successors is Sikh, and this label could be claimed by anyone who is learning or studying something. It means a learner or disciple and comes from the Punjabi word *sikhna* (to learn). But, as you know, in practice it is the name used by members of the particular faith which regards Guru Nanak as its founder.

Once we have a name for something we like to know what it means, to be able to define it. 'Define' literally means 'put a boundary around' something. Dictionaries consist of just this—names and definitions. Here is a definition of a Sikh. It is an English translation of the opening paragraph of the Sikhs' code of conduct, a small booklet called the *Rahit Maryada*, which explains how Sikhs should lead their lives. To understand it you need to be familiar with the word **Khalsa**, the name for Sikhs who are committed to the discipline of their faith:

> A Sikh is any woman or man who believes in Akal Purakh (God), in the ten Gurus (from Guru Nanak to Guru Gobind Singh), in the Guru Granth Sahib, other writings of the ten Gurus and their teachings; in the Khalsa initiation ceremony of the tenth Guru; and who does not believe in any other religion.*

Others have defined Sikh in other ways. In a British television comedy series, *Goodness Gracious Me*, a Sikh father explains to his son that a **pag** plus a man equals a Sikh. *Pag* (pronounced like the English word 'pug') is the Punjabi word for turban, so a Sikh is a man wearing a turban. Probably it is this picture more than any other that comes to people's minds when they hear the word Sikh.

In fact, for many people, Sikh means a person who has five identifying marks. These include having hair which is never cut—hence the turban to cover it smartly and securely. Sikh history reports a day in 1699 when Guru Nanak's last successor, Guru Gobind Singh, performed a simple

---

* In the definition of a Sikh the words 'woman' and 'man' are in the order that they come in the original Punjabi. In Indian languages you would write '*Srimati Srī*' i.e. 'Mrs and Mr' not 'Mr and Mrs'. Does it matter in which order one refers to men and women?

ceremony involving a sword and a bowl of sweetened water and gave his followers new names and a new uniform. He called them his Khalsa (people who belonged only to their Guru). The uniform is known as the ***panj kakkar**** or five Ks as each of the required items starts with that letter. Here is a list of them. You will notice that mostly they are practical items. For Sikhs they also have a strong symbolic value.

kesh uncut hair to preserve our God-given human form. (Can you think of other religious traditions where long hair is looked upon as a sign of dedication? Sikh men (and some women) cover their hair neatly with a turban, one of the most recognisable marks of a Sikh).

kangha a small wooden comb which keeps the hair tidy and symbolises discipline and clarity of mind

kachhahira similar to shorts—considered a practical undergarment, and also symbolic of sexual restraint. (These are referred to in many books as *kachh* or *kacch*, spelt in a variety of ways.)

kara a steel or iron bangle worn on the right wrist, reminding the wearer of God's strength and infinity

kirpan small sword which symbolises freedom and justice

Can you think of reasons why a religious community might need its own special name? Why might it be necessary to look distinctive? (Think of uniformed professions like nurses.) Does this contradict anything earlier on in this chapter? This is the view of a young Sikh woman:

> "I used to be a bit of a rebel and think that if my values were universal I didn't need the label 'Sikh'. Now I realise that humans need to feel rooted and committed to something. You can still have a universal outlook while remaining quite distinct."

* *Panj* means five: in fact Punjab (Panjab) means five rivers (i.e. the tributaries of the river Indus which flow through this area). Punch (originally a drink mixed from five ingredients) is basically the same word. It is also related to the Greek '*pente*' and so to "pentagon".

Is it possible to be proud of your own label and identity and at the same time to avoid judging and stereotyping other people? (Stereotyping means making assumptions about 'all Irish', 'all Asians', 'all teenagers' etc., without thinking of people as individuals with their own characteristics).

Some of Guru Nanak's hymns have been inspired by his observations of distinctive groups of people—for instance pious Muslims and, as in the following verse, members of various Hindu sects:

> Let contentment be your Yogi* earrings;
> Let modesty be your pouch and begging bowl;
> Let meditation be the ashes you religiously wear;
> Let consciousness of death be your head-covering;
> Let pure living be your vow of celibacy
> And faith in God your staff.
> Accept all humans as your equals
> And let them be your only sect.
> Conquering your mind, you conquer the world.

What point is Guru Nanak making?

You could compare this with some words which one of Jesus's early followers, after St Paul wrote in his letter to the people of the city of Ephesus (now in Turkey), 'Put on the full armour of God... the belt of truth...the breastplate of righteousness...the shield of faith...the helmet of salvation...the sword of the Spirit...'

Could you write a few lines about the sort of person you would like to be, using images from a particular group. For instance if you chose doctors or nurses you could use images like 'the stethoscope of careful listening'. You may like to try adding to the following list:

Nurses   e.g. the bandage of sympathy or the syringe of unwanted advice
Cricketers   e.g. the pads of preparation
Chefs   e.g. the seasoning of a sense of humour or the pepper of quick-wittedness

* A *yogi* (yes, the word is related to 'yoga') is an individual who practises an extreme physical discipline which is intended to advance him or her spiritually. In India in Guru Nanak's day (as now) 'holy men' including yogis are recognisable from their appearance. Some yogis of his time were known for their huge earrings which split their ears.

Guru Nanak in Kashmir. In what ways does the appearance of Guru Nanak differ from more recent portrayals shown in this book? Notice his head covering and the forehead mark. The latter is generally associated with the Hindu tradition. From what you have read in this chapter, why do you think images of Guru Nanak might have changed?

Chapter 7: Are we all equal?

What does equality mean to you? It is a word that is used time and time again to represent a great social ideal which we still seem to have trouble achieving. So much so that perhaps we hear the word 'inequality' more often, with reference to the discrimination against minorities or anyone who does not fit a given norm.

What does it mean to say we want to be treated equally? Perhaps you've wanted a parent or guardian to treat you with just as much love and attention, or give you just as much freedom, as they have to a brother or sister. Just because you might dress differently, or listen to different music, or are of a different age or sex, you might think you are being treated unfairly. It may be that we want to be treated equally without having to be the same as someone else.

Guru Nanak's absolute insistence on the Oneness of God went hand in hand with an insistence that we are all equal as God's children. There was no notion of his followers being a 'chosen people', or that all human beings needed to live their lives in the same fashion. Indeed, the extent of Guru Nanak's travels, his meetings with people of many beliefs and cultures, showed a bold openness to diversity and difference. As we have seen in other chapters, Guru Nanak was primarily concerned with people's integrity, inner spirituality, and sense of social responsibility.

Guru Nanak returned from his travels to spend his last years in the Punjab, setting up a community in a village which is now in Pakistan, very near to the border with India. The village was called 'Kartarpur' meaning 'the place of the Creator'. Here his followers were involved in a daily discipline of meditation, singing and manual work, such as farming, preparing and serving food.

Sikhs today aim to perpetuate the principles of Guru Nanak's Kartarpur community, particularly in the *gurdwaras* (places of worship). Here equality can be observed, both practically as well as symbolically, in the following ways:

- men, women and children of any background are made welcome.

- in the worship hall, men and women sit on the same level on either side of the *Guru Granth Sahib*, the holy book, symbolically representing Man and Woman as equals before God.

Cartoon versions of stories from Indian mythology and history are popular. Most famous are the publications called *Amar Chitra Katha* which means (in Hindi) illustrated stories that never die. This illustration conveys the principles on which the Kartarpur community was based.

- at the end of a service, **karah parsad** (a doughy sweet) is distributed to everybody present as a sign of sharing.

- in the **langar** hall and kitchen, the area where free food is cooked, served and eaten, men and women of all social standings collaborate (unpaid) to prepare food, serve and clean.

The *langar*—everyone is treated as equally important.

- people sit and eat on the same level (usually cross-legged in rows on the floor)—there are no special or privileged seating arrangements.

In this way, all people are equally able to carry out **simran** (remembering God) and **seva** (this rhymes with 'flavour' and means selfless service).

Guru Nanak is often praised for 'abolishing the Hindu caste system and making men and women equal'. He valued people regardless of their social standing. However, he did not insist that people should completely reject their traditional roles, either as men or women or as members of a particular caste.

It is perhaps partly because of more recent movements such as Marxism and Feminism, that Guru Nanak is often presented as if he was a 20th century social revolutionary. When you read about individuals who lived in a different period of history or a different society from your own, you need to ask yourself whether there are signs that the way they are presented has been influenced by ideas and words prevalent in another period or culture. What Guru Nanak did, rather than concentrating on the externals of social inequality, was to emphasise people's ultimate spiritual equality.

Like Hindus and many others today Guru Nanak accepted that we all have more than one life on earth, and that our series of rebirths will come to an end only when (through our efforts to follow the path which the Guru showed and by God's grace) we are 'liberated' or achieve *mukti* (the Punjabi word for this liberation). The social status of someone's family—and their caste—has, Guru Nanak stressed, absolutely no relevance at all to the most important goal of human life.

Where do you stand on the following questions:

- If people have spiritual insight, won't they naturally respect everyone as an equal?

- If you were trying to make society more just, would it be more effective to make laws or to change people's hearts?

Chapter 8: Does integrity matter?

If you have Sikh friends, you may notice that many of their names begin in the same way. For example, Gurinder, Gurdeep and Gurbachan all start with Gur meaning Guru or spiritual teacher. Similarly, Gurdip (which is pronounced as Gurdeep and can also be spelt Gurdeep) means the light (**dip** or deep) of the Guru. Another syllable that is part of many names is **Sat** which means Truth. Satpal, Satvinder, Satinder, Satnam and Satwant all have meanings involving truth. You can check some of these, and a number of others, by looking at the list on page 57 which was downloaded from the internet. In chapter 4 you will have noticed that one of Guru Nanak's ways of describing God was **Satnam,** the One whose name is True. Another way in which he referred to God was as **Satguru,** the true spiritual guide.

In some *gurdwaras*, one of Guru Nanak's verses from the *Guru Granth Sahib* is prominent:

> Highest is truth. Higher still is truthful living.

What do you think this means? One way of understanding Guru Nanak's words is that living an honest life is more important than truth in the abstract. Principles are only of value when put into practice. Practise what you preach. The English word for the quality of living in a way that is thoroughly consistent with your ideals is *integrity*. This is the opposite of having double standards, or hypocrisy.

Guru Nanak stressed the importance of our thoughts and wishes as compared with what others see of us from the outside. According to the *janam sakhis* Guru Nanak once burst out laughing while the prayer leader at the mosque, the **qazi** (pronounced 'car' 'zee'), was reciting a prayer. On completing the prayers the *qazi*, who had noticed Guru Nanak's apparently inappropriate behaviour, asked his employer, Daulat Khan, how he could hold such a high opinion of Guru Nanak. Daulat Khan turned to Guru Nanak who observed that God could not accept the *qazi*'s prayer. Hearing this the *qazi* asked what offence he had committed and Guru Nanak explained that while he was reciting the prayer his mind was actually on the possibility that his new born filly might fall into the well nearby. Amazed at how accurately Guru Nanak had read his thoughts the *qazi* fell at his feet as a sign of profound respect for him.*

* Just as the *qazi* fell at Guru Nanak's feet, and this continues to be a sign of respect for elders or spiritual teachers in Indian society, so people still show their respect for the Guru by kneeling and touching the floor in front of the *Guru Granth Sahib* with their foreheads.

Sikh Names & Their Meanings

Name	Meaning
Saihaj	Peaceful and equipoised person
Saihajleen	One absorbed in peace and bliss
Sangat	Associating with holy congregation
Sachsuh	One who attains true peace
Sachsev	Servant of Truth, True servant
Sachkeerat	Singing the praises of God
Sachgian	Having the True Knowledge
Sachfev	Truly Godly person
Sachdian	Absorbed in the True One
Sachpreet	The true love, the love of God
Sachman	True at heart
Sachleen	The one absorbed in Truth, in God
Sachveer	Bravely upholding the truth
Sajjan	A dear friend, a righteous person
Sant	Saintly person
Santa	Exalted person
Satsukh	The one in True Bliss
Satkeerat	One who praises the True One
Satgun	Of True merits
Satjeevan	The one living the truthful life
Satnam	One accepting God's Being as True
Satparvan	The one accepted by God
Satrpeet	The lover of the Truth
Satpal	The one who abides by the truth
Satbachan	The one abiding by the Holy Word
Satbir	The True warrior
Satleen	The one absorbed in Truth, in God
Satveer	Bravely upholding the Truth
Santokh	Contented, peaceful, patient

From the Internet:
Sikh names beginning with the letter 'sassa' or 'sussa' (S) and their meanings.

According to the B40 *janam sakhi*, Guru Nanak also demonstrated this disconcerting ability to read other people's thoughts on a visit to the Hindus' sacred river, the Ganges. There he told one pilgrim that, far from being immersed in prayer this man was actually imagining himself selling oil in Kabul, a great trading centre in Afghanistan, and he told another man that, in his thoughts, he was at home chatting with his wife! Do you think that Guru Nanak was simply concerned at their lack of concentration on what they were doing or at the hypocrisy of appearing to be very devout—and wanting to be regarded as devout—when in fact their mind was on something else?

We all experience tension between the ideal of truth and honesty and the pressures to behave more deceitfully. Tara Singh Bains, the Canadian Sikh, recalls from his childhood:

> Father said don't tell lies, be honest: yet I saw instances in which he defied his own rule. He said he wanted truthfulness, yet when you told him the truth he would hit you.

Integrity is often in the news. There is always some fresh story of a public figure—often a politician or a religious leader—whose private life does not match up to the code of practice that he or she calls for in public. If a policeman is caught committing a crime or a Roman Catholic priest has an affair, journalists are likely to be interested in circulating the news because of the double standards involved.

Another word which Guru Nanak used for 'true' is **sach** or *sacha* (which rhyme with 'much' and 'much-ah'). Notice how many of the Sikh names listed on page 57 begin with this syllable. In Guru Nanak's *Japji*—after the words that are translated on page 30 he emphasises that God:

> was True in the beginning
> is True now
> and shall be True forever.

God is eternal and is uniquely true. People can be true if they focus their thoughts on truth, worship truth and act in accordance with truth. He said:

> The boat of truth is boarded with the help of the divine Guru.

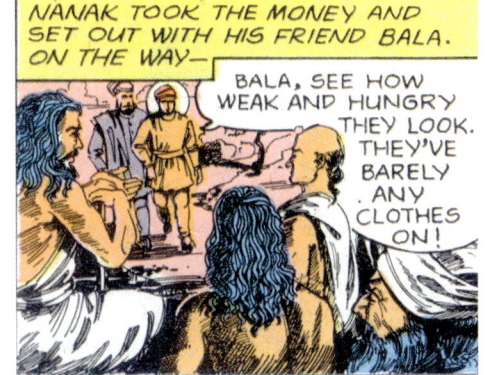

Sacha Sauda: 'the true bargain', from *Amar Chitra Katha* comic.

One *janam sakhi* story suggests that what is true is different from self-interest or common sense. In Punjabi the story is called *Sacha Sauda* or A True Bargain:

According to tradition, when Guru Nanak was about eighteen his wife and parents were anxious because, rather than earning a living, he spent his time with people who had opted to devote their lives to spiritual progress. Instead of getting involved in business, like other *Khatris*, he seemed to be lost in trances and day dreams. One day his father, Mehta Kalu, gave his son's companion, Bala,* some money and instructed them to use it to buy some goods for resale at a profit—a true bargain. But when the two friends were only about ten miles from their village, Talvandi, Guru Nanak spotted in the forest a group of religious renouncers [individuals whose discipline included giving up everything including clothes so that they depended on the support of others]. Turning to Bala, Guru Nanak said, 'Nothing can be more truly profitable than to provide food and clothing for these needy hermits.' With these words he offered the renouncers the money that his father had given them. However, their leader explained that as they stayed in the forest money was of no use to them. So Guru Nanak and Bala went to the next village, paid for food and clothes to be prepared for them and these they gladly accepted. When the two friends got back to Talvandi, Bala told Mehta Kalu how they had used the money—on a true bargain, but Mehta Kalu was angry that his money had been wasted.

Sachkhand (the realm of truth) is another of Guru Nanak's expressions.** In the *Japji* he describes how humans can make progress in their spiritual lives from one stage to another. Truth is an even higher realm than the realms of duty or knowledge.

Closely associated with truth and integrity is the principle of justice, and Guru Nanak had a keen sense of this. According to tradition Guru Nanak spoke out fearlessly against the oppression that the invading Babar (the first of the Mogul Emperors) inflicted as his army killed the people of Punjab, looted and destroyed their homes and carried away their women. The Guru's readiness to speak the truth and suffer the consequences is illustrated by the picture of Guru Nanak serving time labouring in prison. (p.61).

* Out of respect Bala is known as Bhai Bala by Sikhs.

** *Sachkhand* is a term also used for the special room in a *gurdwara* in which the *Guru Granth Sahib* is laid to rest at night.

Guru Nanak in prison during Babar's rule. Innocent of any wrongdoing, he decried the unrighteousness of the times.

Chapter 9: Do we need a sense of direction?

Did you make any new year resolutions this year? Are you the sort of person who has goals—to do well in science, to play for your country, to be a solicitor or to meet your favourite singer in person? Sometimes our parents and teachers have different targets for us from the ones which we set ourselves. Is it important to have something worthwhile to strive for?

When society changes for the better, it is usually because some individuals have had a strong sense of direction and devoted all their efforts to bringing about a particular change. When you look at the lives of two people who campaigned for black people to have equal rights—Martin Luther King in the United States of America and Nelson Mandela in South Africa—you realise what a difference the vision of determined individuals can make to millions of people.

If you look at religious groups—Christians, Hindus and Muslims, for instance—you find teaching about the direction our lives should take, like helping those in need. You will also find that direction in the more literal sense of the points of the compass is taken seriously by many people. For example, Muslims face Mecca when they pray and many Christian churches have their main altars at the 'east end'. Priests conducting Hindu rituals may insist on facing in a particular direction.

There are two *janam sakhi* stories about Guru Nanak which show his attitude to rules like this: one relates to Islam, the other to Hindu tradition.

The picture on page 39 shows Guru Nanak on his way to Mecca. When Muslims pray anywhere in the world they position themselves with their heads facing in the direction of the holy city of Mecca and this is the direction indicated in all mosques by a niche in the wall. Observant Muslims would not knowingly lie or sit with their feet pointing towards this niche as this would be very insulting. Once pilgrims have arrived in Mecca they turn towards the **Ka'ba**, a building believed to have been originally constructed by Adam. Despite the fact that only Muslims are allowed to enter this area, Guru Nanak was admitted and indeed led others in the **namaz** (Muslim prayers). However, on one occasion the *mullah* (the attendant in the mosque) found him asleep with his feet pointing towards the *Ka'ba*. Distressed and indignant he reprimanded Guru Nanak whose response was 'Lay my feet in whatever direction is not God's house'.

Was lying down in the way he had a deliberate 'acted sign'? Certainly his words make his point strongly: God is everywhere and no direction is more sacred than another. But the story continues —as the *mullah* swung his feet round so the *Ka'ba* itself moved in line with them!*

For Hindus the river Ganges is especially sacred and, as you saw in chapter 5, some Hindu rituals involve long deceased members of the worshipper's family. Along with other pilgrims Guru Nanak went into the water to bathe - this is believed to cleanse the bather spiritually as well as physically. Everyone else was following centuries-old practice by facing the rising sun and throwing water in that direction, but Guru Nanak began to throw water to the west instead. Puzzled onlookers enquired if he was a Muslim (as Mecca is west of India) but we are told that Guru Nanak assured them he was Hindu. (Guru Nanak's followers are called Sikhs but the Guru himself was "Hindu" in the sense of having been born into a Hindu family). The people asked

Guru Nanak at Hardwar (*Amar Chitra Katha*)

*   After reading the story of Guru Nanak at Mecca don't be misled into thinking that in a *gurdwara* it is acceptable to sit with your feet pointing towards the *Guru Granth Sahib*!

In the gurdwara the *Guru Granth Sahib* is the central focus of the worship hall and everyone faces in this direction.

him, if this was the case, to whom he was throwing water. He turned the question back on them and they told him, 'We are throwing the water to our ancestors in heaven.' Guru Nanak asked them how far away heaven was and whether the water would get there. They assured him that it would, so he began throwing a large quantity of water to the north west. In answer to their questions he explained 'I am watering my field at home!'

What conclusions can you draw from this story? You will need to think about it again in chapter 11. Certainly Guru Nanak was not constrained by customary feelings of reverence for particular places or directions.

But two words that he used show that in another deeper way Guru Nanak was very concerned about direction. The words are: **gurmukh** and **manmukh** (the '*man*' rhymes with 'one', not with English 'man'). *Gurmukh* means facing towards the Guru/God. So you can make out that *manmukh* will mean facing towards the '*man*'. *Man* is often translated into English as mind, but it carries the meaning of our individual misguided whims and fancies, so the person who is *manmukh* is self-willed. The priorities of *manmukh* people are wrong, so that their lives are at the mercy of instincts like anger, greed and pride. Some other people's lives point like the needle of a compass towards all that God stands for. These *gurmukh* individuals are not self-centred but open to the Guru's teachings about how things really are.

Sikhs believe that they have daily access to the Guru in the form of the volume of Scripture, the *Guru Granth Sahib*. If people are unsure what to do, they can take their bearings from the Guru. The volume is opened at random and the hymn at the top of the left hand page is regarded as the Guru's ruling.

Two friends, Owen Cole and Piara Singh Sambhi, have probably written more than anyone else in Britain today about the Sikh faith. They retell what happened in 1920 when a large number of 'untouchables' (people from the castes that suffered most discrimination from higher caste people) were initiated into the Sikh community. In traditional Hindu society higher caste people would not only not eat with members of these castes, but they would avoid eating any food that they had cooked or handled. The new converts went to the Golden Temple to offer **karah prashad**, the sweet wheat flour pudding that is distributed to everyone in the *gurdwara*. Some Sikh voices were raised in protest at the idea of receiving *karah prashad* from untouchables, whereas reformers insisted that it could be given by all *Khalsa* (initiated) Sikhs. In order to resolve the difference of opinion all parties agreed to heed the Guru's advice, so the *Guru Granth Sahib* was

Opening the *Guru Granth Sahib* for guidance and direction.

randomly opened and the words of Guru Amar Das appeared as the ruling, which began with the words:

> 'Upon the worthless God bestows grace, if they will serve the True Guru...'

Heeding this ruling the higher caste Sikhs dropped their objection.

Do we need a sense of direction? Muslims use a special compass to know the direction of Mecca. The *Qur'an* provides them with a code of conduct. Sikhs can turn to the *Guru Granth Sahib* for advice. Many of us have a person—a relative, friend or counsellor—who helps us to stay on course. Many people have a book: the *Bhagavad Gita* (a spiritual teaching followed by many Hindus), the Bible or books about diet, exercise and how to become rich or happy are examples of the range of reading that people turn to for guidance. When people lose their sense of direction, of purpose and of what is right and wrong, we may say that they have gone off the rails. If your friend needed help in making a difficult decision what would you suggest he or she did?

Chapter 10: How important is wealth?

> Kings with kingdoms vast as the sea
> With riches piled mountain-high
> Are not equal to the tiniest insect
> Who doesn't forget God in her heart.

This statement and others in the hymns of Guru Nanak make it clear that true richness does not lie in outward wealth, although this has its place as you will see later in this chapter.

As you have already discovered, in Indian society some families still follow particular occupations from generation to generation, and there were far fewer exceptions to this in Guru Nanak's day. A farmer's son would be a farmer and a shoe-maker's children could not decide to be goldsmiths, potters or businessmen. This was a key feature of the caste system. Guru Nanak's family belonged to the caste (or *zat*) of *Khatris*, which means that they specialised in accountancy. Money and property were important matters to them, and the *janam sakhis* make it clear that Mehta Kalu, his father, was frustrated and irritated by his son's failure to take money as seriously as he would have wished.

Perhaps because of his family background, Guru Nanak's poems often refer to wealth, but not in a literal way. In the poem below Guru Nanak uses the imagery of a goldsmith in his forge minting coins to express his idea that understanding of the Guru's word (or revealed teaching) is the result of living a disciplined life of intelligent integrity.

> In the smithy of self-control
> Let patience be the goldsmith,
> With wisdom as the anvil
> And knowledge as the hammer.
> Let the fear of God be the bellows,
> Let austerities be the fire,
> Let the love of God be the crucible,
> Let the nectar of life be melted in it.
> In this way, in the mint of Truth,
> The Word is coined.
> This is the practice of those blessed ones
> On whom God looks with favour.

Nanak says, those who receive this gaze are exalted.

Incidentally, notice how much more punchy the original words are, as these two lines show:

>Bhanda bhao amrit tit dhal
>Ghariai sabad sachi taksal

Read the words aloud and imagine the hammer pounding the metal on the anvil to the rhythm of these lines.

Guru Nanak frequently uses images of wealth and treasure to convey the pricelessness of the Guru's teaching:

>The mind sparkles with jewels, rubies and pearls
>If one listens to the teaching of the Guru.

He also urges us to think of life as a precious gift for us to cherish and not waste:

>Life is like a diamond
>Which you have exchanged for a cowrie shell.

To remind yourself of Guru Nanak's attitude to possessions look back at earlier chapters of this book. As a boy he invested his father's money in food for religious beggars and as a young man he accepted the job of keeping the records of Daulat Khan's stores, but gave this up and gave away all he owned after his experience in the river. The accounts in the *janam sakhis* of his conversations with two wealthy men, Duni Chand and Malak Bhago, leave no doubt of his decisive message to his followers about wealth:

1. Money is nothing to be proud of.
2. Money cannot go with us when we die.
3. Money must be earned through honest labour, not by extortion or dishonesty.
4. We should give away anything we do not need to those who do.

It is important to realise that Guru Nanak rebuked some of the conspicuously religious people of his time, who claimed to have renounced the world but in effect became beggars, dependent on other people's charity. Indeed he taught that everyone should work and this should go side by side with remembering God's name. And by distributing what we have wisely, we can make our communities more supportive.

Sikhs have a six word summary of this teaching:

> **Nam japo, kirt karo, vand chhako.**
> Repeat God's name, do your work, share.

They also speak about **dan** (which rhymes with 'yarn') and *seva*. These mean 'giving' and 'serving' without any payment. If you visit a *gurdwara* you will see people leaving offerings (of money, milk or other items) in front of the *Guru Granth Sahib* and doing voluntary work—cleaning, cooking, serving food. The principles of *dan* and *seva* apply to the whole of life, not just to what goes on in a particular building.

So far you have been reading what Guru Nanak's attitude to wealth was - but what is yours?

Donation box in a gurdwara. The woman is kneeling to show respect to the *Guru Granth Sahib* (not shown in picture). Donations may include money and food for the *langar* (see p.54).

You may think that it is unfair that some people are so much better off than others or that some countries are so much wealthier than others. Does the solution lie in individuals deciding to put Guru Nanak's principles into practice in their own lives or in campaigning, e.g. lobbying MPs, for changes in the system? Should we be doing both?

Or you may think that the goal of life is success and the reality is the survival of the fittest: what individuals should do (and are doing) is to compete for resources for themselves and their immediate families.

Which of the points that are numbered 1 to 4 on page 68 do you agree with? What difference would it make to your life if you put these into practice? If you disagree with any of these points, what is the reason? Do you disagree because they are too hard to carry out? Do you expect a different standard of behaviour from your friends and family, or from teachers, neighbours or business people, from what you expect of yourself? In the society that Guru Nanak knew ill-gotten gains were the result of stealing or of exploiting the poor by levying high taxes or lending money at very high rates of interest. Can you think of any other ways in which people today are financially unscrupulous?

Whatever conclusions you reach, remember that in Guru Nanak's view, any preoccupation with wealth (either accumulating it or giving it away) is secondary to life's true focus on the reality of God.

Chapter 11: Rituals and institutions - are they a help or a hindrance?

What comes to mind when you read the words 'ritual' and 'institution'? Probably ritual conjures up patterns of behaviour which are repeated in the same way by individuals and groups of people. Very likely you think of formal religious ceremonies—like marriages. 'Ritual' may seem to be the opposite of being spontaneous or original. Or it may bring to mind occasions that are richer in colour and music than ordinary daily life is. 'Institution' too suggests something established—perhaps an organisation like the Bank of England or the Church of England or a well-worn custom like going to the pub.

Guru Nanak and the world's other great spiritual teachers seem to be part of a contradiction. They publicly and dramatically went out of their ways to challenge rituals and defy institutions. (Think of how Jesus deliberately broke Jewish rules for keeping the Sabbath.) But these same personalities are chiefly remembered by millions of people who have for centuries been involved in the rituals and institutions that have been set up in their names.

For example, pilgrimages are an obvious feature of religious practice. In Guru Nanak's lifetime, just as today, Muslims made their way to Mecca if at all possible and Hindus would come to India's sacred rivers, especially the Ganges, for significant religious acts—for instance for the rites that follow a relative's cremation, which include giving a fee to *Brahmins*. Look back at the stories about this in chapter 9 and decide what Guru Nanak's attitude was to religious convention and time-honoured custom.

There are other stories too: one is about the **janeu** or sacred thread which Hindu boys of high caste start wearing at a special ceremony. On the appropriate day for Guru Nanak's *janeu* ceremony the *Brahmin*, Pandit Hardial, began to put the thread around the boy's neck but he interrupted, asking him , 'What is the use? What authority will this thread give me?' To these questions the **pandit** replied, 'You get spiritual birth by wearing this thread, you can take part in religious rituals—without it you will be impure and cannot perform the annual rite of feeding your ancestors by feeding *Brahmins*; this means that your ancestors in heaven will suffer hunger and thirst'.

Guru Nanak then pointed out, 'If wearing this results in spiritual birth, then the thread should go round the soul. What is the use of wearing it if the wearer goes on lying and back-biting?

People should become compassionate, contented and truthful as a result of wearing the *janeu*—if you have a thread like that I am ready to put it on..' At this the *pandit* protested that this custom had been going on for centuries and no-one else had refused to wear the *janeu*.

Guru Nanak was drawing attention to the greed of some *Brahmins* who performed these rituals as well as questioning the usefulness of wearing the *janeu*. There are other lines too in which Guru Nanak seems to be pointing out that religious custom sometimes perpetuates hypocrisy and double standards rather than encouraging integrity.

But in chapter 6 you saw how conventions of dress and distinctive ways of worshipping also provided inspiration for images in his poems. Sometimes the message is a moral one—for instance on page 141 of the *Guru Granth Sahib* you would find lines of encouragement to lead a sound life. These are inspired by the sequence of five daily prayers which Muslims perform:

> Five prayers, five times a day,
> With five different names:
> Let the first prayer be truth;
> The second: to earn your daily bread honestly;
> The third: charity in the Name of God;
> Fourth: purity of the mind;
> Fifth: the adoration of God.

Both here, and in another famous poem, Guru Nanak is using the Muslim's daily religious routine to flag up what he thinks are even more important: qualities like compassion and honesty. He is not condemning ritual outright, but he is putting it in perspective.

Ritual also moved him with wonder at the world's beauty. Here is a translation of lines which were inspired by the Hindu ritual of **arati** (pronounced a bit like 'arty' but with a clear 'r' sound). You may have seen Hindus expressing their devotion to God in the form of Krishna or the Goddess, for instance, by holding a lamp (a burning wick in a holder) and circling it clockwise (often on a round metal tray) in front of the appropriate picture or **murti** (statue of a deity). At the same time they burn incense sticks, ring a bell vigorously and sing enthusiastically. The **chauri** is a traditional fan, made of horse or yak tail hair in a special holder. In past centuries, before electric fans and air conditioning, kings and other very important people would have an attendant to wave the *chauri* over them in the heat. In this way it has come to symbolise authority, as ordinary people would not have such an attendant. Hindu priests in the temple honour the deities by waving the *chauri* and when the *Guru Granth Sahib* is open a Sikh will wave the *chauri* above the volume—you can see a *chauri* in the pictures on pages 25, 27 and 64.

Guru Nanak saw the processes of the whole universe as an act of unending worship, and composed the following verse which Sikhs recite each night. In this celebration of creation, can you spot the elements of the *arati* ceremony?

> The sky is your silver tray,
> The sun and moon your oil wick lights,
> The galaxy of stars are the pearls that stud it,
> The sandalwood is your incense.
> Your *chauri* is the breeze,
> Wild flowers lie at your feet as offerings.
> O destroyer of fear,
> What a wonderful *arati* this is.
> Unstruck music is the sound of your temple drums.

If you think about it, musical notes are the result of the impact of one thing on another. With percussion and stringed instruments this is obvious, but wind instruments too are silent until air is blown into them. So 'unstruck music' is a deliberate contradiction in terms. It refers to the paradox of 'the sound of silence', the music of God's name, for those who forget outside distractions in meditation.

Guru Nanak composed hymns which his followers sang (and later gathered into a book), and he started **dharamsalas** (places for religious gatherings) in the places through which he travelled, and, as we have seen in chapter 7, started a community at a place called Kartarpur. He also went on to appoint a close follower (whom he renamed Angad) to be Guru after his death. You will find him referred to as Guru Angad Dev.

In these ways Guru Nanak himself provided a basis for Sikhs' institutions and rituals. Present-day Sikh institutions include the *gurdwara* (the place for worshipping as a congregation in which the *Guru Granth Sahib* provides the focus for everyone's attention) and the **langar** (the word is used for the provision of a free vegetarian meal to anyone who comes to the *gurdwara*, and for the kitchen where it is prepared and the area where it is eaten). If you need a reminder

Night sky - an inspiration for Guru Nanak's *arati* poem.

of the significance of these institutions for Sikhs, look back to chapter 7. *Langar*'s original meaning is anchor—one way of looking at institutions is as anchors which keep society steady. We speak too of needing our moorings. Sikh rituals include a distinctively Sikh marriage ceremony (**anand karaj**) and the procedure for choosing a baby's name. In each case it is the presence of the *Guru Granth Sahib* which is vital.

If you are not a Sikh, you may belong to another religious community or you may feel that you have no links with any religion at all. But, whatever the case is, you will still find that there are rituals and institutions that figure in your experience. Think of terms like 'the English breakfast' and 'the great British weekend'. Think of school and youth clubs and football matches as well. Nightclubs too are institutions that lead individuals to behave in a particular set of ways which might not be appropriate somewhere else. Think of the different ways people generally behave in a post office or a pub, a class room or a hospital. Would some behaviour that is acceptable in one of these places strike you as odd in another?

Guru Nanak's teaching poses questions for every one of us. One of these is: How can rituals and institutions help us to be better human beings? In other words, how can they help us to put into practice the principles of love and compassion, truth and honesty and serving other people? If they are more of a hindrance than a help, then Guru Nanak's advice is clear! Some of the institutions that you have considered are intended for recreation, some are widely regarded as characteristics of a country's culture, others are means of keeping useful public services running efficiently.

What criteria would you use in deciding whether they are worthwhile?

A night-time reading of the *Guru Granth Sahib*

Chapter 12: How can we sum up Guru Nanak's message?

As you look back over previous chapters of this book what stands out as Guru Nanak's central insight and teaching? In chapter 8 we looked at his insistence on integrity, a consistency between principles and practice. In chapter 3 we saw how the nature of God, or of what is ultimately true —the subject of millions of spoken and written words—can be communicated in just 12 words (the *mul mantar/mul* [pronounced 'mool'] *mantra*).

Here is one of the fundamental questions posed by Guru Nanak, which occurs in one of the opening lines of the *Japji Sahib*, and comes at the very beginning of the *Guru Granth Sahib*.

> How can one be true?
> How can we break the veil of deception?
> By attuning ourselves to the Will,
> Says Nanak, this is written for us.

Soon after comes the statement:

> Nanak says, by recognising the Will
> We silence our ego.

If you look back in this book to the episodes recounted from Guru Nanak's life and examples of his teaching, you will see that his main concern was with the way a person was responsibly aware of all his or her thoughts and actions. He was keen to expose, sometimes humorously, sometimes quite dramatically, how human beings, when driven by their own ego, can delude themselves. If we begin to recognise the Will (i.e. God's will, *hukam*—see chapter 3) and see ourselves in the greater scheme of things, rather than as being in the centre of our own worlds, we can lead our lives with a sense of harmony and understanding.

As we have seen, Guru Nanak's recipe for attaining this state is threefold. Let's take a look again at the formula which was mentioned on page 69.

Nam japo

Remember the Name: through meditation we can practise attuning ourselves to the truth. By doing this regularly, we can keeep ourselves 'in tune', rather like a musical instrument, and we can develop a constant awareness of the Name.

Kirt karo
Work: by leading a life of action, and not just of silent meditation, we can experience life in a fuller way. There is a sense here of 'earning our daily bread', an attitude which encourages self-sufficiency rather than a lazy dependency on others!

Vand chhako
Share with others: by doing this we become responsible and supportive human beings, making our own inner spirits generous as well as offering outward practical help.

Like people of other communities Sikhs are fond of mnemonics, memory aids—often single words which remind us of a lot more. You can probably think of mnemonics that you have used during revision for examinations. The threefold formula that we have just looked at is a mnemonic, reminding Sikhs of Guru Nanak's message.

If you visit a *gurdwara* try and see ways in which it is set up to be a practice ground for these principles. Nowadays Sikhs will often refer to *seva* (selfless service) and *simran* (meditation) as the two underlying principles.

Seva (pronounced say-vah)	Help others.
Simran (pronounced simrun)	Remember God.

For Sikhs *seva* firstly suggests working as a volunteer in a *gurdwara*, especially preparing and serving food, and *simran* particularly means remembering God by repeating (*japna*) one of the names which Sikhs give to God, like Vahiguru or Satnam. More generally *seva* can mean helping other people, whatever the circumstances, and *simran* can mean keeping our scampering thoughts focused on what we believe to be most true. By practising *simran* we can learn to become more constantly aware of the *Nam*.

Neither requires any special qualifications and Sikhs believe that both offer transformation to everyone who is willing to persevere. Guru Nanak offered no instant techniques for perfect living or express tickets for enlightenment; *simran* and *seva* need to be practised daily. Musicians and athletes will understand how daily practice can help us realise our potential. Like the seed which the farmer plants and nurtures, our spirituality and humanity need to be cultivated.

Finally, rather like the farmer who depends on good weather—toil as we may we cannot succeed

'My meditation on Guru Nanak' by Sobha Singh

without good fortune and God's grace. Guru Nanak constantly reminds us of this in his hymns, and the *mul mantar* ends with the word 'Gurprasad', which is often translated as 'through the Guru's grace'. We would be wise to remember that ultimately any success is not completely in our own hands.

There is much that has not been covered in this book, but we hope that it has given you enough glimpses into Guru Nanak's life and teaching so as to enable you to follow up clues by reading more about him.

We also hope it has helped convey why Guru Nanak is such a central figure in the hearts and minds of Sikhs the world over, and why he continues to receive veneration and praise from people in all walks of life.

Chapter 13: Why end with thirteen?

Do you belong to a culture in which the number 13 can produce a faint shudder, even if this is tinged with amusement or embarrassment at a foolish superstition? There are roads with no house numbered 13, and some people make wry jokes about events due to be held on a Friday if it is also the 13th.

For Guru Nanak's followers, by contrast, the number 13 has very positive connotations, all because of a Punjabi pun.

You will remember that as a young man Guru Nanak was employed as a storekeeper for the wealthy Daulat Khan Lodhi. Nanak's job involved weighing out grain in a pair of scales, and counting up the number of times the scale pans were filled. But whenever he was counting and reached the number 13 he would stop concentrating on the job in hand and become overjoyed with the thought of God, repeating the word 'tera' (13) over and over again. To understand the point of this story you need to know that in Punjabi 'tera' also means 'yours'.

In the midst of his day to day commitments and distractions Guru Nanak was overwhelmed by the sense that everything is Yours (i.e. God's) as everything arises from God and is in God's keeping.

Glossary

(Help with pronouncing some terms is given in the text. 'a' is pronounced either as 'er' or as the vowel in 'far'; 'i' resembles either the vowel in 'fill' or in 'feel' and 'u' is always either like 'u' in English 'pull' or 'oo' in 'pool'.

anand karaj	the Sikh marriage ceremony.
arati	Hindu worship involving moving a flame in a circle in front of a respected person or an image of God.
bani	utterance, the Guru's word, the *Guru Granth Sahib*.
bhai	brother. Title showing respect or familiarity.
caste	a community associated with a particular occupation. Membership is hereditary and some castes are respected more than others.
chapati	flat, circular, yeastless bread, freshly baked on a griddle.
chauri	a fan, made from horse hair. By waving this over the *Guru Granth Sahib* Sikhs show their respect for its authority.
dan	giving
dharamsala	the earlier term for a gurdwara, the place where Sikhs gather to worship. In India the word more generally means very basic accommodation for travellers.
dip/deep	a lamp consisting of a small clay saucer, a wick made by twisting cotton wool and purified butter (ghee).
gurmukh	devoted to the Guru, devout.
gurdwara/ gurudwara	Sikhs' place of worship.
hukam	will, especially God's will.
ik	one in Punjabi
janam sakhi	collection of stories of Guru Nanak's life.
janeu	(jun oi) a stranded thread which Hindu men of high caste are entitled to wear.

japna	to repeat
japo	repeat!
kachhahira	(cutch-air-rah) shorts, one of the five Ks (see below) worn by Khalsa Sikhs.
kangha	wooden comb, one of the five Ks.
kara	a circular steel wrist band, 'bangle', one of the five Ks.
karah parsad/ prashad	mixture of wheat flour, water, sugar and butter which is distributed during Sikh worship.
kesh	(almost like 'case') hair, one of the five Ks (refers to hair and beard allowed to grow untrimmed in accordance with Khalsa discipline).
kirpan	sword, one of the five Ks.
kirtan	singing of hymns from the scriptures in worship.
langar	the free, corporate vegetarian meal available for anyone who attends a gurdwara or Sikh religious ceremony. The term also applies to the area where this is cooked and eaten.
manmukh	opposite of gurmukh. A wayward person.
mukti	liberation - especialy from the cycle of transmigration. You may also find the Sanskrit term, moksha.
mul mantar	literally 'root formula', Guru Nanak's statement of belief.
murti	a three-dimensional image of God used as the focus of Hindu worship.
nam/Nam	name—in the sense of God's name this is a key concept for Sikhs. Nam means the reality of God.
namaz	the obligatory Muslim prayers.
oankar	(ੴ) the syllable om, conveying the reality of God (also omkar, onkar)
pag	turban

pandit	a Brahmin, the priest conducting a ceremony; a learned person.
panj kakkar	5 items beginning with K and essential to the discipline of a Khalsa Sikh.
pothi	book
qazi	a Muslim official.
rabab	a stringed instrument.
rag(a)	a combination of musical notes which provides the basis for composing South Asian music.
sach/sacha	true
sat	true
satnam	the True Name, a way of referring to God.
seva	voluntary service, a fundamental principle for Sikhs.
shabad	literally a word, a musical rendering of a passage from the scriptures.
sikhna	to learn
simran	to remember, especially remembering (repeating) God's name as a form of religious devotion.
tabla	a pair of finger drums.
tera	thirteen; your
untouchable	name formerly used for members of the castes which suffered most discrimination.
vaja	harmonium
yogi	a Hindu who has devoted his/her life to extreme spiritual and physical discipline.
zat	a caste: a hereditary group associated with a particular occupation. Members are expected to marry someone from the same zat.

List of Names and Pronunciation Guide

A guide to pronunciation follows most words (in brackets). Literal translations are given in the second brackets.

Adi Granth	(aadi grunth) (original volume) the Sikhs' scriptures.
Akal Purakh	(akaal purkh) (timeless person) God.
Alam Chand Raj	(rhymes with culham, chaand raaj) the illustrator of the manuscript now called the B40 janam sakhi.
(Guru) Amar Das	(rhymes with summer daas) (1479-1574) third Sikh Guru.
Amritsar	(Um rit sur) (pool of nectar) city in Punjab (India) famous for the Golden Temple, Sikhs' most respected place of worship.
(Guru) Angad Dev	(un-gud dave) (1504-1552) second Sikh Guru.
Arabic	the language of the Muslim scriptures. Arabic numbers are the numerals now used most widely throughout the world.
(Guru) Arjan Dev	(charge-un-dave) (1563-1606) fifth Sikh Guru.
Asa	(aasaa) one of the 31 *rags* (musical measures) to which the hymns in the Adi Granth are sung.
B40 (*janam sakhi*)	name given to a 17th century manuscript of stories of Guru Nanak (ie a janam sakhi) in the India Office Library, London.
Baghdad	present capital of Iraq. Visited by Guru Nanak according to tradition.
Bala	(baalaa) according to popular belief Bhai Bala was Guru Nanak's companion. In pictures he is often shown fanning the Guru.
Bein	see Vein
Bhagavad Gita	(rhymes with hug a card neater) (song of the Lord) a Hindu scripture, focusing on duty and devotion. Lord Krishna's sermon in the Mahabharata epic.
Bhago	(bhaago) see Malak Bhago

Bhumiya	a robber who became Guru Nanak's follower.
Brahmin	the Hindu caste (hereditary community) to which priests belong.
Daulat Khan Lodhi	(dowlut khaan loady) Guru Nanak's employer.
Daya Ram Abrol	the scribe who copied out the B40 janam sakhi manuscript.
Duni Chand	a wealthy man who became Guru Nanak's follower.
Eminabad	(Eh-meaner-baad) a small town in Punjab - see map.
The English Patient	award-winning novel (later film) by Michael Ondaatje.
Ganges	(Ganga in Indian languages) a major river of North India, sacred to Hindus.
Gurdas	(the u as in pull) (c1558-c1637) Bhai Gurdas was both theologian and poet.
Guru	teacher, spiritual guide. For Sikhs the term refers to God, the ten human Gurus and the scriptures.
Guru Granth Sahib	Sikh scriptures, a volume consisting of hymns.
Gurumukhi/Gurmukhi	(the 'u's as in pull) the script of Punjabi and of the scriptures.
Hardwar	(hurdwaar) Hindu pilgrimage place on the bank of the Ganges river.
Sir Mohammad Iqbal	(1877-1938) famous Muslim poet.
Japji	(rhymes with up we) (repeat [God's name].) Guru Nanak's much-loved composition on pages 1 to 8 of the *Guru Granth Sahib*.
Ks	five identification marks—all starting with K—of a Sikh who observes the discipline expected of a Khalsa member. See glossary for *kachhahira, kangha, kara, kesh, kirpan*.
Ka'ba	the focus of Muslim prayer in Mecca.
Kabir	(cub eer) (c1414 - 1518) saint-poet. Of the hymns in the *Guru Granth Sahib* that were not composed by the Gurus, Kabir's are most numerous.

Kartarpur	(kar-tar poohr) town in Gurdaspur, Punjab, founded by Guru Nanak.
Khalsa	(khaalsaa) Sikhs who have been initiated in a ceremony involving holy water and who follow a strict discipline including the five Ks.
Khan	title of a Muslim nobleman.
Khatri	(cut-ree) the largely urban, hereditary (caste) community traditionally involved in trade and banking.
Krishna	a popular Hindu deity, an incarnation of God Vishnu.
Lakhmi Das	(luck me daas) Guru Nanak's younger son.
Lalo	(Laalow) Bhai Lalo was the carpenter whom Guru Nanak commended.
Malak Bhago	(mar luck bha go) Lalo's wealthier fellow villager whom Guru Nanak condemned for exploiting the poor.
Mardana	(murdaanaa) Bhai Mardana was Guru Nanak's Muslim musician and companion. His descendants (Muslim musicians) still perform the Guru's hymns.
Mecca	Muslims' holiest place of pilgrimage, Makkah.
Mehta Kalu	Guru Nanak's father.
Mohan Pothis	(mow-hun, pothis rhymes with note he's) collections of the first three Gurus' hymns. These belonged to Baba Mohan, the third Guru's elder son, and became the basis of the *Guru Granth Sahib*.
(Guru) Nanak	(1469 - 1539) (Naa nuck—NB neither 'a' rhymes with 'a' in the English word 'man') first Sikh Guru. 'Shri' (before his name) and 'Dev' and 'Ji' (both after his name) are usually added as marks of respect.
Pakistan	since 1947 an independent country on India's north-west border. More of Punjab is in Pakistan than in present-day India.
Pandit Hardial	the Hindu priest who tried to conduct the thread ceremony for Guru Nanak.
Plato	(428/7-328/7 BCE) Greek philosopher who has significantly influenced European thought.

Punjab	(rhymes with one barb) the land of five rivers, now divided between India and Pakistan.
Qur'an	(Koran) Muslim scriptures
Rai Bhoi di Talvandi	(raaee bhoee dee tulvundee) Guru Nanak's birthplace, now in Pakistan and known as Nankana Sahib (see map).
Rahit Maryada	Sikh code of discipline, a booklet containing this.
Ramanand	(raam aanund) north Indian religious teacher, one of whose hymns is in the *Guru Granth Sahib*.
Ramkali	(raam-cull-ee) eighteenth of the 31 musical measures (*rags*) used in the scriptures.
Randhir Singh	(run-dheer) (1878-1961) Bhai Randhir Singh was a devout Sikh campaigner for India's independence from Britain. He interpreted Khalsa requirements very strictly and is particularly respected by Sikhs who belong to the Akhand Kirtani Jatha.
Sacha Sauda	(rhymes with such a powder) (true bargain) Guru Nanak's giving of money to feed some people who had devoted their lives to religion rather than investing it for financial profit.
Sanskrit	the ancient Indian language in which many Hindu scriptures are written.
Satguru	('a' like 'u' in 'but') (true guru) this term is used of both God and Guru Nanak.
Satnam	(sut-naam) (true name) God's name is true, a word frequently repeated in prayer.
Sikh	(usually pronounced 'seek' by English-speakers, more correctly the vowel 'i' is short as in 'is') (learner) a follower of the ten Gurus.
Siri/Sri Chand	Guru Nanak's elder son.
Sobha Singh	(1901-1986) eminent Sikh artist most famous for his portraits of Guru Nanak.
Sri	(shree) Respectful title.

Sri	a *rag* (musical measure) used in the *Guru Granth Sahib*.
Sulakhani	(u as in pull, luck knee) the wife of Guru Nanak.
Sultanpur	(the 'u's are as in 'pull', tan as 'tarn') the town in Punjab where Guru Nanak was employed (see map).
Talvandi	see Rai Bhoi di Talvandi.
Tripta	the mother of Guru Nanak.
Urdu	a language related to Hindi and Persian and written in Arabic script.
Vahiguru	(originally meant: praise to the Guru) God.
Vein	(also Bein) the river into which Guru Nanak disappeared at the time of his enlightenment.

Acknowledgements

First and foremost we would like to thank Ram Krishan Prashar, Harbhajan Singh and Jaswinder Kaur Panesar, Avtar Singh Thethy and all dear friends for their help and support during the making of this book. We are also grateful to the copyright holders, authors, artists and publishers of all material reproduced in it. Every effort has been made to identify and contact the copyright holders of artistic work for permission. Any omissions will gladly be rectified in future reprints. For 'My meditation on Guru Nanak' by Sobha Singh (cover and p.79) from the Government Museum and Art Gallery, Chandigarh, and for "Guru Nanak and Bhai Laloji' (pp.44-5) by Bhodhraja from Baba Baghel Singh Museum, Bangla Sahib Gurdwara, New Delhi, we gratefully acknowledge Aravali Books International (P) Ltd, New Delhi. For 'Guru Nanak' by Sobha Singh (p.8) donated by Ms Randhawa, we acknowledge the GNPS Trust. For the pictures on p.14 & p.61 from 'Guru Nanak', by PM Wylam, we are thankful to the Guru Nanak Foundation, New Delhi. In the absence of a traceable copyright holder for the image on p.17, we acknowledge Bebe Nanaki Gurdwara, Sultanpur, Punjab. We thank Harpal Singh for permission to reproduce his pencil drawing on p.18. The illustrations on pp.21, 39 and 51 (A Magnate, Baba Nanak and Mardana F188V; Baba Nanak and Mardana with Fakirs on their way to Mecca F132; Baba Nanak and Mardana in Kashmir F159R) are reproduced by permission of The British Library from the B40 Janam-Sakhi (India Office Library Gurmukhi Manuscript Panj. B40). For the image on pp. 24-5, we acknowledge SS Brijbasi & Sons, Karachi. Twin Studio is gratefully acknowledged for permission to use Guru Nanak's Enlightenment (p.29) and The Pool of Immortality (p.32). We acknowledge W.H. McLeod's Popular Sikh Art (Delhi, Oxford University Press, 1991) for 'Guru Nanak ploughing' by Anil Sharma on p.34. For the illustration on p.38, we are grateful to Jaswant Singh and the Indian Museum Art Gallery, Chandigarh. Sandeep Brar is thanked for 'Sikh names' taken from The Sikhism Home Page website (www.sikhs.org), reproduced on p.57. The illustrations on pp.53, 59 and 63 are reprinted with permission from Amar Chitra Katha, India Book House Ltd. 1998. Baldev Singh Thethy is thanked for kind permission to use his photograph on p.54. The photographs on pp.27, 41, 46, 64, 66, 69, 76 and 80 were taken by Gopinder Kaur in West London at the Sri Guru Amar Das Gurdwara and Sri Guru Singh Sabha Gurdwara, Southall, and the Central Gurdwara, Shepherds Bush, and the picture on p.35 in the Punjab. Grateful thanks goes to all those who have appeared in them.

Books quoted or referred to:

Bains, Tara Singh and Johnston (1995) *The Four Quarters of the Night: The Life-Journey of an Emigrant Sikh*, Montreal and Kingston, McGill-Queen's University Press, p.7 (quoted in chapter 1), p.231 (quoted in chapter 2).

Cole W.O. and Sambhi, P.S. (1995) 2nd ed *The Sikhs: Their Religious Beliefs and Practices*, Brighton, Sussex Academic (chapter 9 refers to pp54-5).

D- (1998) an untitled poem in *The Big Issue*, 9 (3) quoted in chapter 3.

de Mello, A. (1990) *Awareness*, London, Fount. Page 48 is quoted in chapter 6.

Ezard, John (1998) 'Soothing, arresting: classical music for head bangers', *Guardian*, 3 Nov (referred to in chapter 5).

Gates, Brian (1976) *The Language of Life and Death: Religion in the Developing World of Children and Young People*, unpublished PhD thesis, University of Lancaster (referred to in opening paragraph of chapter 1).

Iqbal, Muhammad (1969) 'Nanak' in Ganda Singh (ed) *The Punjab Past and Present 3 (1 and 2), Guru Nanak's Birth Quincentenary Volume, Sources of the Life and Teachings of Guru Nanak*, Patiala, Department of Panjab Historical Studies, Punjabi University p.9 (quoted in chapter 1). For translating the Urdu for us we thank Mr Said Akbar of Coventry, UK.

Jagdev, Santokh Singh (1992) *Bed Time Stories II (Guru Nanak Dev Ji)*, Birmingham, Sikh Missionary Resource Centre (In chapter 11 the *janeu* story comes from here).

McLeod, W Hew (1969) 'The Life of Guru Nanak according to Bhai Gurdas' in Ganda Singh (see above) pp.32-4 (quoted in chapter 1).

McLeod, W Hew (1980) *Early Sikh Tradition: A Study of the Janam-sakhis*, Oxford, Clarendon. (story of rich money-lender in chapter 2 is based on McLeod's translation).

McLeod, W Hew (1980) *The B40 Janam-Sakhi*, Amritsar, Guru Nanak Dev University (The story of the *qazi* in chapter 8 is based on p.22-3 of this translation. The other examples of mind-reading are from p85-6.).

Ondaatje, Michael (1993) *The English Patient*, London, Picador, page 271 is quoted in chapter 5.

Singh, Trilochan (1971) (trans) *Autobiography of Bhai Sahib Randhir Singh*, Ludhiana, Bhai Sahib Randhir Singh Publishing House, p xiii (referred to in chapter 3).

In our renderings of passages from Guru Nanak's compositions we have been especially helped by four translators:

Duggal, Kartar Singh (1997) *Select Sikh Scriptures 1 Guru Nanak*, Birmingham, DTF.

McLeod, W Hew (1984) *Textual Sources for the Study of Sikhism*, Manchester, University of Manchester Press.

Singh, Nikky-Guninder Kaur (1995) *The Name of my Beloved: Verses of the Sikh Gurus*, San Francisco, HarperSanFrancisco.

Singh, Trilochan *et al* (3rd impression 1973) *Selections from the Sacred Writings of the Sikhs*, London, Allen and Unwin.

Stories of Guru Nanak/janam sakhis
N.B. *Janam sakhi* stories are not readily available in English through mainstream book outlets as they have either been published in academic studies such as those by McLeod (see above) or as stories for younger children, usually published by Indian or Sikh publishing houses. Two collections are:

Jagdev, Santokh Singh (1992) *Bed Time Stories-II (Guru Nanak Dev Ji)* Birmingham, Sikh Missionary Resource Centre, ISBN 1 872580 21 1. (Punjabi and English).

Singha, H.S. and Kaur, S. (rep 1997) *Sikh Studies Book V Guru Nanak Dev*, New Delhi, Hemkunt Press ISBN 81-7010-247-2.

Quotations from the *Guru Granth Sahib* (*Adi Granth*) are from the following - the page numbers refer to the *Gurmukhi* text which is used in worship. All titles except *Japji* denote the musical *rag* to which they are sung, which determines their position in the text.

p.7	'One may read cartloads of books'	—Asa (p.467)
p.16	'If like a bird'	—Sri (p.14-15)
pp.30,58	'There is one being'	—Japji (p.1)
p.31	'Air is our guru'	—Japji (p.8)
p.33	'If my body were a vat'	—Tilang (p.721)
p.33	'Make your mind the plough'	—Sorath (p.595)
p.35	'You are like the ocean'	—Sri (p.25)
p.50	'Let contentment be your Yogi earrings'	—Japji (p.6)
p.56	'Highest is truth'	—Sri (p.62)
p.58	'The boat of truth is boarded'	—Sri (p.20)
p.67	'Kings with kingdoms vast as the sea'	—Japji (p.5)
p.67	'In the smithy of self-control'	—Japji (p.8)
p.68	'The mind sparkles with jewels'	—Japji (p.2)
p.68	'Life is like a diamond'	—Gauri-Bairagan (pp.156-7)
p.72	'Five prayers'	—Majh (p.141)
p.73	'The sky is your silver tray'	—Dhanasri (p.13)
p.77	'How can one be true?'	—Japji (p.1)

A Note for Teachers

As well as being intended for a wider public, it is hoped that this book will be used with pupils of varying abilities aged 13 to 18 in Personal and Social Education classes, general Religious Education, and examination level (GCSE and 'A' Level) Religious Studies groups. Throughout the book, in keeping with the SCAA model syllabuses, the principles of learning from, as well as learning about, faith traditions have guided the authors. Issues relating to the reliability of sources also connect to the history syllabus.

The questions that occur in the text provide a basis for discussion and for written work—for example, 'Does life have a meaning?' Pupils can be asked to discuss this in small groups and then write their response in prose or verse form. After reading the chapter they can discuss what they think the basic 'rule' of the universe, or at least of this planet, or of human society is—e.g. God is love, survival of the fittest etc.

Ask pupils to look attentively (in groups) at the pictures of Guru Nanak. They can then list the ways in which these convey Guru Nanak's significance to those who met him and for people today. Advise them to look out for detail such as the sign ੴ and at the composition of the picture —for example the size, posture and position of Guru Nanak in relation to other individuals, whether there is a canopy (natural—such as the spreading branches of a tree—or otherwise) over his head or an attendant fanning him—both signs of respect for an authority.

Ask pupils to imagine meeting Guru Nanak and hearing him express his insights. They may choose one of the specific incidents recounted in this book if they wish. Suggest that they produce a newspaper report. This could be for a religious paper e.g. a Roman Catholic, Hindu, Jewish or Muslim one. In this case they will need to reflect on how what they are reporting relates to readers of that particular faith. (They may decide to write for members of a group which did not exist at the time of Guru Nanak e.g. Methodist or Bahai or for readers who are critical of religion e.g. Humanists).

Alternatively, pupils can be asked to write a detailed entry in their diary for the day when they first encountered the Guru and his teaching.

Suggest that pupils set about designing an interactive CD-rom or a website on Guru Nanak. What pages will they include, bearing in mind the importance of Guru Nanak not only as a historical figure but also in Sikh life today?

If they have worked through the book as a whole, pupils may use the Glossary and List of Names as the basis of a quiz to check their knowledge/understanding of the contents of the book.